Guilty or Not, Here I Come

John Nicholas Schweitzer
4713 Regent Street
Madison, WI 53705
(608) 231-3941

SCENES

The author's image of this play is as follows, but it need not dictate the actual set. The left half of the stage starts as the living room of Pat's and Sam's home, and it remains so for most of the play, doing double duty only as the district attorney's office. The right half of the stage changes to become the police station, the courtroom, the public defender's office, the private attorney's office, and the processing area of a jail.

ACT I

ACT II

TIME

The day before yesterday, or the day after tomorrow.

CAST

Character	Scenes (1-20)
Pat Barlow	1-20
Sam, Pat's Wife*	1-5, 7, 10, 12, 15, 17, 19
Police Officer	1, 17
Police Receptionist	2
Detective Perez	2
First Denizen	4, 6, 8, 13, 18, 20
Judge	4, 8, 13, 18
Public Defender Receptionist	6
Second Denizen	13
Attorney†	6, 9, 11, 13, 14, 16, 18
Second Attorney†	6, 13
Assistant District Attorney	4, 8, 13, 14, 16
others in courtroom	4, 8, 13
Jailer	20

----

* The play is written around a conventional heterosexual marriage relationship, which will be most familiar and most acceptable to some. However, each role, even Pat, was conceived as potentially being played by a person of either gender. Third-person pronouns and words such as Mister/Miss, Ma'am/Sir, wife/husband (or significant other), and shirt/blouse may be adjusted at the director's discretion to suit the cast. All the characters may be either male or female, and other than Pat, the pronoun "she" is used throughout but may be changed as appropriate to accommodate the cast.

† Attorneys that practice private criminal defense would very seldom be waiting in the Public Defender's Office, and the two attorneys who appear in scene 6 are acknowledged anomalies. Having the First Denizen appear in scene 6 is also literary license, since s/he is not represented in the courtroom scenes, but it is not totally implausible, as s/he could be in the Public Defender's Office for another charge.

ACT I
Scene 1. Pat's and Sam's Home

[The curtain rises on a dark stage. Lights partially up on the left half of the stage, a living room with a sofa, an easy chair, lamps and tables, a phone and a clock. A door stage left leads to the outside and doors on the back wall lead to the bathroom and to the kitchen. Some movement may be seen and heard onstage, which is Sam stirring on the sofa.]

SAM
Is that you, Pat? *[Sam turns on a lamp and looks around. She has been sleeping on the sofa.]* Are you home? *[Sam yawns, stretches and reaches to turn out the light, then stops. She sits motionless for a moment, picks up the clock, looks at the time, and sets it down again. After another moment of indecision, Sam stands up, turns on the room lights-- at which the lights go fully up on the left side of stage--picks up the phone, looks at a number affixed to the side, and dials.]* Hello. No, this isn't an emergency. At least I hope not, but ... OK, I can hold. Hello. I called a couple of hours ago ... Well, can you just tell me if you've had any reports of ... *[Pat has approached the door and now makes some noise opening it.]* Wait. Oh, it's OK, he's home now. Thanks anyway. Bye. *[Sam hangs up and jumps up as Pat comes through the door.]* You're home. *[They hug.]* Are you okay?

PAT
Yeah, I'm okay.

SAM
I was so worried about you. *[Sam hugs him again.]* Are you sure you're all right?

5

PAT
Yeah, I'm sure.

SAM
I called the police every hour or so.

PAT
I'm sorry.

SAM
So where were you.

PAT
At the party, Arin's party. You remember, don't you?

SAM
All night?

PAT
Nooo. I can tell you where I was until about two a.m., but after that I don't remember.

SAM
You don't remember?

[Beat.]

PAT
No.

SAM
Who were you with.

PAT
Uh, some people I met in the bar. You wouldn't know them.

SAM
And what were you doing between two and now.

PAT
I told you. I don't remember.

SAM
Really? You must remember something. *[Long pause.]*
Well?

PAT
I really don't remember much at all except the early part of
the evening.

SAM
Okay, then tell me what you remember, and we'll go from
there.

PAT
Arin's going-away party at the Laurel Tavern. It was a good
party, but I must've lost track of time and the number of
drinks I had, 'cause after the cards and the gifts and the
speeches ... not really speeches, but, you know, maybe
toasts, a lot of 'em ... the next thing I remember is noticing
it's closing time and I looked around for a familiar face and
they were all gone. They must've all left without me. *[Long
pause.]* And then I was outside with some people I didn't
know and somebody had a twelve-pack and we just stayed
there, I don't know how long.

SAM
You didn't stay there the whole night.

PAT
[Hesitantly.] No.

SAM
What kind of people were they.

PAT
What kind of people?

SAM
Were there both guys and girls?

PAT
Oh, yeah. *[Pause.]* I think so.

[Long pause.]

SAM
So after the parking-lot party?

PAT
I don't remember. I don't remember what I did or where I've
been. *[Pause.]* I woke up in the back seat of my car a little
while ago. I had a terrible headache -- still do -- and then I
drove home.

[Pause.]

SAM
So where was the car when you woke up, in the parking lot?

PAT
[Slowly, as if thinking is painful.] No, it was parked on the
side of the road.

SAM
You drove like that?!

PAT
I guess so.

SAM
You could've killed somebody, or yourself.

PAT
I guess ... I guess my judgment was impaired.

SAM
Along with your memory.

PAT
Yeah.

SAM
So you don't remember what you did, other than use very
bad judgment and do things you'd never do when you're
sober. No, I won't go there, not now. Why didn't you call.

PAT
I guess I didn't want to bother you, or wake you.

SAM
Not bother me! Pat, I was waiting up for you forever, and
then, if I slept, it wasn't much. You said you'd be home by
midnight.

PAT
Did I say that? Well, it wasn't a promise; it was just a ...
prediction.

SAM

And I told you to call me if you were going to be late, or if
your plans changed. Midnight, even one o'clock, I expected,
but after that, I got worried. By three o'clock, I was worried
sick about whether you were hurt or dead, or ...

PAT

I was okay.

SAM

I can see that! And I'm so glad you're home safely.

PAT

I ... Sam, I'm sorry. You know I sometimes drink more than
I should. Once I start, I don't always know hoe to stop.

[Beat.]

SAM

So after you left the parking lot, where'd you go.

PAT

I don't know! The memory's not there. Honest. I must've
had a heluva lot to drink. I was so drunk, I couldn't put my
wallet back ... *[Beat while he remembers.]* There was a cop.
That's right, she woke me up in the car when I was sleeping
and she asked if I was all right. She asked for my drivers
license, and I remember pulling out my wallet for an ID and
then having a lot of trouble putting it back. I hope I still
have it. *[Pat reaches for his wallet, finds it and pulls out a
drivers license.]* Thank goodness.

SAM

So where were you. Where was the car then.

10

PAT
I was ... I was over on Atwood Avenue. *[A street a mile or so further from their home than the street on which the crime is supposed to have occurred.]*

SAM
But that's not on the way home from the Laurel.

PAT
No, it isn't.

SAM
What were you doing over on Atwood.

PAT
I don't know.

SAM
Pat, I've tried really hard not to worry about anything except whether you were all right. And I don't want to make a big deal of it. Not now.

PAT
I don't think I did anything really bad, except worry you. I just drank too much and forgot everything, including you, and I'm sorry. *[Pat touches Sam's arm.]* Sam, really I am.

[Pat embraces Sam, who acquiesces stiffly. Sam touches Pat's sleeve.]

SAM
What's this.

11

PAT

What. Is it mud? No, it's ... it looks like blood. *[Pat pulls up his sleeve and looks at his arm.]* I don't see anything. *[Pat feels his head and face.]* Is there anything on my face?

SAM

Nothing visible.

PAT

Maybe I had a bloody nose.

SAM

You don't remember this, either? *[Pat shakes his head.]* Take off your shirt.

[Pat does. Sam checks him.]

PAT

Do you see anything?

SAM

No. So you're all right?

PAT

I guess so.

SAM

Then ... it's somebody else's. *[Pause while they look at each other.]* Did you get into a fight?

PAT

I don't think so.

SAM

Do I believe you? *[Pause.]* I don't know. Well, at least

you're home and I can stop worrying about the simple
questions like whether you were run over by a truck. Maybe
we can move on to the more complicated ones later. Why
don't you take a shower and go to bed for awhile. I'll rinse
this and throw it in the washing machine. Maybe it won't
stain too badly. And maybe later you'll remember more.

PAT
Okay.

*[Pat goes into the bathroom area offstage while Sam takes
the shirt and exits through the kitchen door. Noises off
indicating water running, first from the bathroom, then from
the kitchen. The kitchen noise stops. Sam returns,
straightens things, goes to the bathroom door and is just
about to open it when there is a knock at the front door.]*

SAM
Just a minute! *[Sam goes to the door and opens it.]* Oh.
Good morning, officer.

POLICE OFFICER
May I come in?

SAM
Uh, sure. *[The police officer enters.]* You must've traced
my call. It's okay now, really. My husband came home
safely. I'm not wild about the fact that he stayed out all
night, but at least he's home safely now. Come in.

POLICE OFFICER
What call was that, ma'am.

SAM
Isn't that why you're here, because I called?

13

[The sound of the shower stops.]

POLICE OFFICER
I'm afraid not. Did you call the police?

SAM
Yes. I was worried when my husband didn't come home, but it's okay. He's here now.

POLICE OFFICER
Well, that's good, because I need to talk to him.

SAM
Did he get into some sort of trouble last night?

POLICE OFFICER
Did he?

SAM
I don't know. I just know he was out all night.

POLICE OFFICER
I need to ask him some questions.

PAT
Who are you talking to!

SAM
A cop, a police officer. She wants to ask you some questions.

PAT
Just a minute.

14

SAM
Would you like to sit down?

POLICE OFFICER
No thanks.

[Pat enters in a bathrobe.]

PAT
Good morning, officer. Excuse my appearance, but you
caught me in the shower. Did something happen last night?
I'm afraid I won't be much help. I really don't remember
seeing anything unusual. In fact, I don't remember much at
all, but if you can tell me what you're after, maybe I'll be
able to remember something.

POLICE OFFICER
Are you Pat Barlow?

PAT
Me? Sure. Yes, I am.

POLICE OFFICER
Date of birth 7-27-72? *[A date to make Pat about 30.]*

PAT
Yes.

POLICE OFFICER
And this is your residence?

PAT
Yes. What is this.

15

POLICE OFFICER
Your wife tells me she was waiting up for you all night.
When did you arrive home?

PAT
About fifteen or twenty minutes ago.

POLICE OFFICER
We'd like you to come down to the station to give a
statement.

PAT
About what.

POLICE OFFICER
If you don't mind, the detective will ask the questions and
you'll give the answers, and it's not my job to put words in
your mouth or ideas in your head. Do you know where the
police station is?

PAT
Sure.

POLICE OFFICER
Can you be there in half an hour?

PAT
Half an hour? I guess so.

POLICE OFFICER
When you get there, just ask for Detective Perez.

PAT
But ...

POLICE OFFICER
Yes?

PAT
Nothing, I guess. I'll be there.

POLICE OFFICER
By the way, where are the clothes you were wearing last night.

PAT
They're in the bathroom, where I took them off.

POLICE OFFICER
Would you mind letting me look at the shirt and pants?

PAT
I'll get you the pants, but my wife has the shirt.

[Pat exits and returns with the pants. The officer looks at the color and style and writes something in a notebook. She turns questioningly to Sam.]

POLICE OFFICER
Ma'am, the shirt, please.

SAM
I'm afraid the shirt's all wet. I was rinsing it.

POLICE OFFICER
Why is that.

[Beat.]

SAM
It was dirty.

POLICE OFFICER
May I see it anyway?

SAM
Sure.

[Sam leaves and returns with the damp shirt. The police officer looks it over and writes something in a notebook.]

POLICE OFFICER
Is there any particular reason you were washing it already?

SAM
Well ... it was dirty, and some things need to be rinsed out quickly or they can stain, like red wine.

POLICE OFFICER
Was there red wine on the shirt?

SAM
I'm not sure what it was, but it could've been.

[The officer writes.]

POLICE OFFICER
And you just took a shower, is that correct?

PAT
Yes.

[The officer writes again.]

POLICE OFFICER
Thank you. By the way, would you like to buy a raffle ticket
for the police and firemen's ball?

[Pat stares at her with disbelief.]

SAM
Uh, not now, thanks.

POLICE OFFICER
Okay. Good-bye.

PAT & SAM
Bye.

[The police officer exits.]

SAM
Do you have any idea what that was about?

[Pat shrugs his shoulders. Sam exits into the kitchen and
Pat exits slowly back to the bathroom. Lights down.]

Scene 2. The Police Station

[Lights up on the right half of the stage. Visible are a reception area and the receptionist, then a separated detective's office and Detective Perez. Pat and Sam enter.]

PAT
Hello. I'm Pat Barlow, and I'm here to see Detective, uh ...

SAM
Perez.

POLICE RECEPTIONIST
Oh yes, just a minute.

[The receptionist picks up a phone and dials. Detective Perez picks it up.]

DETECTIVE PEREZ
Yes?

POLICE RECEPTIONIST
Pat Barlow is here to see you.

DETECTIVE PEREZ
Right. Thanks. Send him in.

POLICE RECEPTIONIST
Mr. Barlow, Detective Perez's office is the first on the left. You may go in now.

PAT
Can my wife go with me?

POLICE RECEPTIONIST
I'm afraid not. She'll have to wait here.

[Pat walks to and enters Detective Perez's office. Sam reads magazines throughout the scene.]

DETECTIVE PEREZ
Mr. Barlow. Have a seat.

PAT
Thank you.

DETECTIVE PEREZ
This is a tape recorder, and I'm going to record our entire conversation, for your protection as well as mine. After we're through, I'll ask you to wait until it's transcribed. You can read it and correct any errors the typist made, and then you should swear to its accuracy and sign it.

PAT
Do you want --

DETECTIVE PEREZ
Wait. I'll turn it on now. *[He turns it on.]* Do you have any questions before we begin the formal statement?

PAT
Yes. Why am I here.

DETECTIVE PEREZ
Why do you think.

PAT
To answer questions.

DETECTIVE PEREZ
Right.

PAT
About what.

DETECTIVE PEREZ
What do you think.

PAT
I guess about something that happened last night. Did
something happen?

DETECTIVE PEREZ
That's the kind of question I ask you, and before we discuss
that I have to inform you of your rights. I meant do you
have any questions about the procedure.

PAT
Yeah, what if I don't want to give a statement.

DETECTIVE PEREZ
Then you're free to go. You're not in custody. Of course, if
you haven't done anything wrong, then you have nothing to
hide, have you.

[Pause.]

PAT
No, I don't. So go ahead.

DETECTIVE PEREZ
First, I have to tell you that ... *[He takes a card out of a
pocket and reads at breakneck speed.]* You have the right to
remain silent. Anything you say can and will be used

against you in a court of law. You have the right to talk to a lawyer and have him or her present with you while you are being questioned. If you cannot afford to hire a lawyer, one will be appointed to represent you at public expense before any questioning, if you wish. If you give up your right to remain silent, and later wish to stop answering questions, no further questions will be asked. Are you still willing to make a statement?

PAT
Sure.

DETECTIVE PEREZ
What's your name.

PAT
Pat Barlow.

DETECTIVE PEREZ
What's your date of birth.

PAT
July 27, 1972.

DETECTIVE PEREZ
What's your address.

PAT
3959 Plymouth Circle, Madison, Wisconsin. *[An in-joke address of someone related to the production or a fictitious address on a street in the city of the performance.]*

DETECTIVE PEREZ
Did you come to the station voluntarily today?

PAT

I guess you could call it that. When a cop says "come here", you come.

DETECTIVE PEREZ

But you weren't forced to come, were you?

PAT

Well, of all the things I could've done this morning, coming here wasn't high on my list.

DETECTIVE PEREZ

But no-one forced you to come here.

PAT

Are you trying to get me to say that I came down here all on my own, because I wanted to talk to you?

DETECTIVE PEREZ

Not exactly, but you're here voluntarily, aren't you?

PAT

No, I'm here because a cop told me to come and talk to you.

DETECTIVE PEREZ

But no-one coerced you.

PAT

Coerced? As in twisted my arm? No. A cop doesn't need to push me to get me to move.

DETECTIVE PEREZ

But --

PAT
Wait, I understand, you can't take your statement unless I say
"voluntarily", right? *[Beat.]* OK, I came here voluntarily,
after a cop told me to, will that do?

DETECTIVE PEREZ
Yeah.

PAT
So let's move on. What's the next question on your list?

DETECTIVE PEREZ
Are you giving this statement voluntarily?

[Long pause.]

PAT
Yes.

DETECTIVE PEREZ
Right. You were at your residence at 6:40 A.M. this
morning when Officer Finley called for you?

PAT
Some cop. I don't remember her name. My wife answered
the door 'cause I was taking a shower.

DETECTIVE PEREZ
Was it 6:40 A.M.?

PAT
I don't know exactly, but that's about right.

DETECTIVE PEREZ
It could've been 6:40 A.M.?

PAT
I suppose.

DETECTIVE PEREZ
So you were at your residence at 6:40 A.M. this morning
when Officer Finley called for you?

PAT
I said I was there when the cop came, but I'm not sure of the
time.

DETECTIVE PEREZ
But it could've been 6:40 A.M.

PAT
Yes.

DETECTIVE PEREZ
Then you were at your residence at 6:40 A.M. this morning
when Officer Finley called for you?

PAT
I was there, but I can't tell you the time.

DETECTIVE PEREZ
But if the officer's report says 6:40, then that's right, isn't it?

PAT
I don't know.

DETECTIVE PEREZ
Would there be any reason for the officer to falsify the time?

PAT
Would there?

DETECTIVE PEREZ
Let's try this again. Officer Finley arrived at your residence
at 6:40 A.M. Were you there when Officer Finley arrived?

[Beat.]

PAT
Yes.

DETECTIVE PEREZ
And what time did you get home.

PAT
Maybe twenty minutes earlier.

DETECTIVE PEREZ
And before that, when was the last time you were at your
residence.

PAT
About 7 A.M. the day before, when I left to go to work.
After work we all went to the Laurel Tavern for a going-
away party.

DETECTIVE PEREZ
What time did you get to the Laurel Tavern.

PAT
About 5:30.

DETECTIVE PEREZ
P.M.?

PAT
You thought I meant A.M.?

DETECTIVE PEREZ
I'm just being thorough.

PAT
I'd call it anal.

DETECTIVE PEREZ
It's my job to cover all the possibilities.

PAT
Next question.

DETECTIVE PEREZ
You didn't answer the last one.

PAT
I told you, 5:30!

DETECTIVE PEREZ
A.M. or P.M.

PAT
Good god, P.M.!

DETECTIVE PEREZ
All right. Now tell me where you went and what you did
between 5:30 P.M. yesterday and, uh, 6:20 A.M. today.

PAT
I was at the Laurel, as far as I know, until at least 2 in the
morning, eating and I guess mostly drinking, and that's when

I noticed that everyone else was gone, everyone I was with.

DETECTIVE PEREZ
And after that?

PAT
I don't know. I really don't know.

DETECTIVE PEREZ
You don't remember four and a half hours?

PAT
No!

DETECTIVE PEREZ
Do you expect me to believe that?

PAT
What is this, an inquisition?! *[Pat speaks loudly enough for Sam to lower her magazine momentarily to listen.]* I'm telling the truth, and I don't know what's going on. What am I supposed to have done wrong.

DETECTIVE PEREZ
I ask the questions; you give the answers.

PAT
Then I don't know anything else. I must've been in a haze for the rest of the night. I have quite a hangover.

DETECTIVE PEREZ
Where were you at 4 A.M.

PAT
I told you, I don't know.

DETECTIVE PEREZ
Were you on Monroe Street between Regent and Adams?
[An address in the city of the performance, where the alleged crime is supposed to have occurred.]

PAT
How should I ... I don't think so.

DETECTIVE PEREZ
Where were you at 5:30.

PAT
A.M. or P.M.

[Beat.]

DETECTIVE PEREZ
A.M.

PAT
Listen, I told you ... At 5:30? I don't know, but I woke up around 6, so I guess I was sleeping in my car, which was parked on Atwood Avenue.

DETECTIVE PEREZ
Did you talk to a police officer then?

PAT
Yeah, I did. I mean, I talked to an officer, but ...

DETECTIVE PEREZ
But what.

PAT
But I don't know what time it was.

DETECTIVE PEREZ
Had you been in any sort of altercation?

[Pause.]

PAT
I don't think so.

[They look at each other for a long time, both trying to
decide how much to say.]

DETECTIVE PEREZ
Why were you in the shower ten minutes after you got home.

PAT
I'd been out all night, and I wanted to clean up and relax and
sleep in my own bed.

DETECTIVE PEREZ
And why were your clothes in the wash.

PAT
It was just my shirt, because it was dirty.

DETECTIVE PEREZ
Are you always so fastidious?

PAT
What?

DETECTIVE PEREZ
I meant, do you always wash your shirts the minute they get

dirty?

PAT
It seemed like ... my wife wanted to ... It was dirty. Sam
wanted to wash it before ... There was a stain on it. It
might've been red wine.

DETECTIVE PEREZ
Was it red wine?

PAT
I don't know. I don't remember spilling red wine or
anything else on my sleeve.

[Beat.]

DETECTIVE PEREZ
Was it blood?

[Long pause.]

PAT
I don't think so. No, it didn't look like blood. No, I'm sure
it wasn't.

DETECTIVE PEREZ
All right. Thank you. *[Detective Perez stops the tape
recorder.]* Please wait out in the reception room. I'll call
you in to sign your statement when it's been typed. You may
go.

PAT
And what if I don't want to sign it.

DETECTIVE PEREZ
You don't have to, but I keep the tape. If I have to use the tape, it just makes the procedure a lot more tedious when we get to your trial.

PAT
My trial!? I thought I was just here as a witness or something.

[Pause.]

DETECTIVE PEREZ
That was an interesting reaction. Too bad it's not on the tape.

PAT
Well, can't you add it on?

DETECTIVE PEREZ
Sorry. That's not the way it's done. *[A sign appears somewhere that says "That's not the way it's done."]* The typist works off the tape. Please wait outside.

[Pat gets up, leaves Detective Perez's office and sits next to Sam with a blank expression. Sam puts her arm around Pat.]

SAM
So how did it go?

PAT
Uh, not good.

[Lights down.]

Scene 3. Pat's and Sam's Home

[Lights up on the left half of the stage. Sam enters through the door stage left. Pat is offstage through the kitchen door. A small pile of junk mail is on a table.]

SAM
I'm home. Are you here?

PAT
You're late.

SAM
I told you this morning I'd be working late. Don't you remember? I said I'd have to work late to cover somebody's route. I said I'd be home before six. It's five-fifty. *[Pause.]* Is this the mail? *[Sam sits and begins to look through the mail.]* How was your day.

[Pat enters from the kitchen, holding a sheet of paper behind him. Sam doesn't notice.]

PAT
I've had better.

SAM
You sound depressed. Was it a hard day at work?

PAT
No.

SAM
You aren't going to have to work the late shift again, are you?

34

PAT
No.

SAM
I give up. What happened.

PAT
How long has it been since ... since that cop showed up at
the door?

SAM
Three or four weeks. Let's see, this Saturday it'll be four
weeks. You aren't still worried about that, are you?
Nothing ever came of it. I figure cops can usually figure
things out, and if they didn't find anything worth following
up on, then there's nothing there. *[Sam looks up.]* Why do
you ask. Did you finally remember something about that
night?

PAT
No.

[Pat holds out the paper.]

SAM
What's that.

PAT
A summons. It was in today's mail.

SAM
For you? For what.

PAT
To go to court.

SAM
For you? I mean, is it ... Does it say you did something?.
[Pat nods.] What ... what does it say you did.

PAT
You don't have to be so excited about it. It doesn't say
anything.

SAM
What do you mean. It has to say something. What are you
charged with.

PAT
I'm not really sure. I think it's disorderly conduct, but there's
a lot more and I can't tell what's important. Look at it.

SAM
Disorderly conduct, contrary to ... what's this.

PAT
That's what I said. There's a squiggle like one of those
Greek letters, but I never saw this one before, and then
there's a number. Who knows what that is.

SAM
Well, you're the one who got the charge. What do you think
it means. You obviously did something.

PAT
Go to hell.

SAM
What's eating you.

PAT
You act as if just getting this paper proves I did something.

SAM
Well, doesn't it? *[Pause.]* Intentionally and unlawfully.
That sounds bad.

PAT
I didn't give you this to laugh at.

SAM
I'm not laughing.

PAT
You're treating it like a joke.

SAM
No, I'm not.

PAT
Well, you're not serious about it.

SAM
How can I be serious about something you claim is all
wrong.

PAT
It's still serious.

SAM
A penalty of one thousand dollars or ninety days
imprisonment. Pat, this is serious.

PAT
That's what I said.

SAM
Did you get drunk and get into a fight and beat somebody
up? Is that what this says?

PAT
I don't know. I don't understand it. This doesn't describe
anything I remember.

SAM
Your aff ... affiant – What's that. It sounds like ... Affiant ...
you aren't engaged to somebody else, are you?

PAT
Come off it.

SAM
Well ... your affiant has read the report of Officer DePere of
the Madison *[name of the city in which the performance is
taking place]* Police Department, whose reports have been
reliable in the past -- Well, that's good. -- and said report
reports she spoke to John Doe, who is reliable as a citizen
witness – Oh, that's good, too. – and who reported that at
approximately 4 A.M. on June seventh, two thousand two
[the year of or preceding the performance], in the city of
Madison *[same as above]*, she observed the defendant, Pat
Barlow, in a public or private place, to engage in violent,
abusive, indecent, profane, boisterous, unreasonably loud or
otherwise disorderly conduct under circumstances which
tended to cause or provoke a disturbance.

PAT
That's certainly helpful, isn't it.

SAM
Is it? Did you do all of that?

PAT
Just go to hell.

SAM
Well, does it trigger your memory?

PAT
No, it doesn't help at all. Besides, the date's wrong. I
wasn't out at 4 A.M. on the seventh. It was the eighth. The
seventh was when the party started. I think the rest of it's all
messed up, too.

SAM
Do you think you should see a lawyer?

PAT
We can't afford a lawyer!

SAM
I know, but if it's serious enough ...

PAT
They've got the wrong date, they've got the wrong person.
I'll go to the first hearing and it'll be thrown out.

SAM
I'll go with you. When is it.

PAT
It isn't for three weeks.

SAM
Why so long.

PAT
How should I know.

SAM
Hang in there. It'll be all right. Let me help you with
supper. What are we having.

PAT
Whatever you want. I haven't even started. I was just sitting
in the kitchen peeling the label off a bottle. I guess I am a
little depressed. Even after cooking all day, I always enjoy
cooking for you, but today I just couldn't get going.

SAM
Come on. Let's make something special together. How
about chicken marsala.

PAT
Sure.

[They exit into the kitchen. Lights down.]

Scene 4. The Courtroom

[Lights up on the right side of the stage, which is now a courtroom, fairly realistic. The assistant district attorney is present. Indistinguishable functionaries and various low-lifes, including the First Denizen, are seated around the room. Pat and Sam enter and take seats as far as possible from the other seated figures.]

PAT
This doesn't look much like the courtroom in Law and Order *[choose the name of a courtroom drama in contemporary entertainment]*.

SAM
Are you scared?

PAT
Scared? No.

SAM
That's good, 'cause I'm intimidated.

PAT
There's no reason to be. I'll just tell them this is all a mistake, and ...

[Beat. Sam puts her hand on Pat's forearm supportingly.]

SAM
And it'll be thrown out of court!

PAT
Right.

SAM
Do you suppose all these people have cases here today?

PAT
Sure, why not. And they're probably all innocent, too.

SAM
No. What do you suppose they all did? Look at that one
over there. I don't like his looks. Do you suppose there's a
child molester in here?

PAT
Don't be melodramatic. I bet they're all here by mistake.

SAM
No way. They didn't just pick up everybody in here off the
street by accident. You can tell just by looking at them.
That one in the corner, doesn't he look like he could murder
somebody?

PAT
Cut it out!

SAM
What.

PAT
Assuming all these people did something just because they're
in court.

SAM
Not you, of course. And maybe not everybody here's guilty.
But just look around at these
losers. Have you ever seen a sorrier bunch of people?

[The First Denizen gets up and sits next to Sam.]

FIRST DENIZEN
So this the first time you ever been in a courtroom?

SAM
How'd you know?

FIRST DENIZEN
I've got a sixth sense, sort of a psychic. I can feel vibrations.
Don't worry, though, you'll get used to it, bein' in court, I
mean.

PAT
What if I don't want to get used to it.

FIRST DENIZEN
Well, what you want don't matter much here. No more'n it's
gonna matter when the real judgment day comes. See that
pulpit up there? That's where the judge sits. And these
pews, this is where we sit until we're called. Y'ever notice
how much a courtroom resembles a church, with a preacher
and us sinners?

PAT
Can your sixth sense tell if somebody's innocent?

FIRST DENIZEN
Can my ... what? Oh yeah, course it can. There ain't a
single innocent person here, especially the lawyers and the
judges, except ... lots of 'em are innocent of the crimes
they're accused of. Get it?

PAT
Of the crimes they're accused of? Oh yeah, I guess so. But

43

that wasn't what I was asking. Can you tell by vibrations or something --

FIRST DENIZEN
If a person's innocent? Are you serious? What're you here for.

PAT
Something I didn't do.

FIRST DENIZEN
Well, then …

PAT
Can you tell whether I'm innocent?

SAM
Pat, she doesn't really have a sixth sense.

FIRST DENIZEN
You really thought I did? You must be in deep. All I meant was I been here often enough to tell the lambs from the lizards, and at the moment, you're a lamb.

SAM
How could you tell this is our first time in a courtroom.

FIRST DENIZEN
It's easy. 'Cause you're paying attention, you're curious, you act like something important's gonna happen, instead of just bein' a place where lawyers and judges and other court-types -- I don't know what they're all called -- do their business while we sit and watch, and wait, and're told to come back again some other day.

PAT
You're right, this is our first time in a courtroom, but it'll also be our last.

FIRST DENIZEN
Ha! Well, if you say so. There's a first time for everything, but what makes you think you're not comin' back.

PAT
The complaint's all wrong. I didn't do anything.

FIRST DENIZEN
That's what we all say, and it ain't worth a nickel here.

PAT
The date's wrong on the complaint. I'll just point that out and they'll dismiss it.

FIRST DENIZEN
I've heard that before. Lemme tell ya, it doesn't slow 'em up a bit. The D.A.'ll just make a motion to amend the charge to conform to the evidence and they keep going as if nobody's supposed to even notice that they just switched direction or switched gears. If I was a gambler – which I ain't -- that's not my vice – mine's just driving when I shouldn't – sometimes, not this time – I'd take any odds this won't be your last time here. Once you're in, you're in.

SAM
How often does this happen.

FIRST DENIZEN
What.

SAM
Court, like this. Once a month?

FIRST DENIZEN
Ha! That's another good one. Every day, five days a week,
eight hours a day, except when the judge comes in late or
wants to leave early.

SAM
I had no idea!

FIRST DENIZEN
People who never get sucked in to the system don't realize
it's even here. Say, have you heard the one about the
attorney and the nun?

SAM
What?

FIRST DENIZEN
Have you heard the one about the attorney and the nun?

SAM
I don't understand. Is that a joke?

FIRST DENIZEN
Yeah. Lawyer jokes. That's one of the things we do to pass
the time here; it's how we greet each other: "Hey, have you
heard the one about the attorney and the nun?" You'll have
your own favorites soon, and your own list of stupid things
lawyers say and do.

*[A white-haired, black-robed judge enters and sits on the
raised "bench". One of the functionaries intones "All rise."
Pat and Sam rise quickly and stand at attention. The other*

46

*defendants stand listlessly. The court types half-rise. The
ADA moves to the counsel table]*

JUDGE
You may be seated. Is this a civil or a criminal calendar.
[She looks around the room.] Criminal, obviously. This is a
calendar call for January, February, March and April.
Herian. Roger Herian. *[This and the following two names
can be those of local persons.]* Non-appearance. Warrant.
All bonds forfeited to the county. Directions to the district
attorney to issue a bail-jumping charge based on non-
appearance. Next. Parker. Hilary Parker. Non-appearance.
Judgment on default. One hundred dollars plus court costs,
city tariff, school tax and parking lot assessment, total seven
hundred twenty-three dollars and fifty-two cents, due in
thirty days or thirty days in jail, whichever comes first.
Barlow. Patrick Barlow.

[Pat jumps up.]

PAT
Here. *[The judge scowls.]*

FIRST DENIZEN
[Leans over and whispers.] Your honor.

PAT
Your honor.

JUDGE
Let's do that again. Pat Barlow.

PAT
Present, your honor, ma'am.

JUDGE
And where is your attorney.

PAT
I ... I don't have one. Your honor.

JUDGE
Don't you want an attorney?

[Pat looks around at Sam and the denizen.]

PAT
I don't really know. I came here to --

JUDGE
You have a right to one.

PAT
I do?

JUDGE
Of course.

PAT
I didn't know that. I thought attorneys were only available if you paid for them.

JUDGE
Well, of course.

PAT
Then I'm afraid I don't understand.

JUDGE
You have the right to pay for an attorney.

PAT
That's a right?

JUDGE
That's right. *[Beat.]* That is, unless you can't afford one.

PAT
Then I don't have a right to an attorney?

JUDGE
No, then you get one free.

PAT
Oh.

JUDGE
Can you afford one?

PAT
I don't think so.

JUDGE
Then contact the Public Defender's Office. They'll tell you if
you qualify. Case adjourned. It will be put back on the
initial appearance calendar for September, April, June or
November. Stantis. Kirk Stantis.

PAT
But excuse me, your honor. There's been a mistake.

JUDGE
Your case has been adjourned. You can discuss it with your
attorney.

[Blackout.]

50

Scene 5. Pat's and Sam's Home

[Lights up on the left half of the stage. The stage is empty. Sam enters through the door to the outside, carrying a grocery bag and some mail.]

SAM
Are you home? *[She puts the mail on a table, and goes in the kitchen and returns without the bag.]* Pat, are you home? *[Mimicking voice.]* No, of course I'm not home yet. I said I'd be home early, so you assumed I'd be home early. Gotcha again. And did I think to call and tell you my plans had changed? Of course not. I never think of you. *[Normal voice.]* I swear, someday I'll get tired of your lack of consideration and walk out. *[She goes to the bathroom door, opens it, and stops in the doorway.]* Oh! You're here. Didn't you hear me? *[Pat is invisible in the bathroom area.]*

PAT
What? Oh. No, I guess I was asleep.

SAM
In the bathtub?! Say, you look nice. How about if I take off my clothes and join you.

PAT
Uh, no. I'm not in the mood.

SAM
Not in the mood? When are you ever not in the mood.

PAT
On a day like today. Let me get out.

SAM

Okay.

[Sam returns to the sofa, sits down, sifts through the mail, picks up a magazine, and starts reading. Pat enters in a bathrobe.]

SAM
What's wrong.

PAT
I was trying to relax.

SAM
Are you upset about your case?

PAT
You think I shouldn't be?

SAM
No, I didn't say that. I just mean is that the reason you're upset?

PAT
I'm not upset.

SAM
I thought you said you were.

PAT
I'm trying to relax. I'm tense.

SAM
Oh. Okay. Whatever you say, but you sure chose a strange way to relax. Do you know what you looked like in there?

PAT
No, and I don't care.

SAM
How long have you been home. The mail was still in the
box.

PAT
I left work just after the lunch rush, said I didn't feel well,
and nothing'll get you out of Denny's kitchen faster than
that.

SAM
So are you coming down with something?

PAT
Naw, I feel okay. I just used that as an excuse. I couldn't
concentrate today.

SAM
Couldn't concentrate. Why. Why not.

PAT
I just keep thinking about my case.

SAM
Did you remember something?

PAT
No!

SAM
No, of course not. So what were you thinking about.

PAT
I was thinking maybe I should be doing something. I don't
know what, but what if there's evidence out there that I didn't
do it, or there's a witness who can say I was somewhere else
when whatever it is happened, and what if by putting it off
for weeks like this that person disappears. I should be doing
something, or the police should be doing something, or a
lawyer should be doing something, but I have no idea what.

SAM
When's your appointment with the Public Defender's Office.

PAT
Next Monday.

SAM
What time?

PAT
Two o'clock.

SAM
That's not a good time for me. I hope you don't mind if I
don't come with you. It's right in the middle of my
downtown run.

PAT
Course not. I didn't expect you to. There's no need for you
to lose half a day. I hope I can finally find out what I'm
charged with.

SAM
Isn't it that violent and abusive thing?

PAT
Disorderly conduct.

SAM
Right. Disorderly conduct. So?

PAT
So I don't understand it. And if that person, that denizen of
the courtroom, was right about them being able to just
amend the charge and change the date, maybe I really need
to start worrying about it. And if I don't understand it, how
can I fight it?

SAM
Well, isn't that what a lawyer's supposed to help you with?
[Pause.] Did sleeping in the bath relax you?

PAT
A little.

SAM
Great. You know, you make me feel cold just looking at
you. *[Sam goes over to Pat and slips her hand inside his
bathrobe or up his leg.]* Should I try to warm you up a
little?

PAT
No! Not now.

[Sam backs off.]

SAM
Okay. Jeez. Why don't you get dressed. I'll start dinner.
Any requests?

PAT
Naw. Whatever.

[Pat exits through the bathroom door.]

SAM
Is that under W in the recipe box? *[Sam exits through the kitchen door.]* I love you, too. I'll see what I can do.

[Lights down.]

Scene 6. The Public Defender's Office

[Lights up on the right side of the stage, which is now the reception area for the Public Defender's Office. A receptionist sits behind a desk near the entrance. The First Denizen sits near the receptionist. Two attorneys stand in conversation. Pat enters and goes to the receptionist.]

PAT
I have an appointment to ... to see if I qualify for Public Defender services.

PUBLIC DEFENDER RECEPTIONIST
Fill out this form.

PAT
Okay.

PUBLIC DEFENDER RECEPTIONIST
Have a seat. When it's complete, return it to me.

[Pat glances over the form, which is many pages long.]

PAT
What if I don't know some of this, like the value of all my assets. I didn't bring my life history with me.

PUBLIC DEFENDER RECEPTIONIST
Fill in what you can. Estimate if you need to. If it's close, we'll ask for verification.

PAT
Okay. Thanks.

[Pat takes a seat as far as possible from the others and

works on the form.]

FIRST ATTORNEY
Judge Richmond was certainly in a pissy mood today.

SECOND ATTORNEY
Oh?

FIRST ATTORNEY
Ever since she was appointed to the bench, she's had a serious ego problem. I think she has trouble now remembering whether she was born in a log cabin or a manger.

SECOND ATTORNEY
It started long before she was appointed.

FIRST ATTORNEY
Well, now she's fallen in love with her own voice.

SECOND ATTORNEY
As if she wasn't in love with it before, when she was a mere assistant D.A.

FIRST ATTORNEY
But now she thinks her every word is golden, and she can compress more words into fewer ideas than any person I've ever known.

SECOND ATTORNEY
She certainly doesn't understand the law. The only thing she understands is investments.

FIRST ATTORNEY
How so.

58

SECOND ATTORNEY
She's the one who turned me on to tax-deferred annuities.

FIRST ATTORNEY
Oh?

SECOND ATTORNEY
Yeah. Don't you know? They're the best investments we can make at our age.

SECOND ATTORNEY
Did she tell you that? My investment counselor doesn't think much of them. I've got my money in stocks, about half blue-chips and half technology.

[Pat stands.]

ATTORNEY
You're more of a risk-taker than I am.

SECOND ATTORNEY
No risk, no return.

[Pat returns to the receptionist with the form. The receptionist simply turns it over and looks at the back of the last page.]

PUBLIC DEFENDER RECEPTIONIST
You have a job?

PAT
Yes.

PUBLIC DEFENDER RECEPTIONIST
At more than minimum wage?

PAT
Yes.

[The others look at him with curiosity.]

PUBLIC DEFENDER RECEPTIONIST
Then your income puts you above the cutoff for Public
Defender services.

PAT
Does that mean I don't qualify?

PUBLIC DEFENDER RECEPTIONIST
No.

PAT
No I don't or no I do.

PUBLIC DEFENDER RECEPTIONIST
You're above the cutoff.

PAT
Is that good or bad.

PUBLIC DEFENDER RECEPTIONIST
Well, that sort of depends on your point of view. If you're
looking --

PAT
Do I qualify for public defender services?

PUBLIC DEFENDER RECEPTIONIST
No.

PAT
Then why did the judge send me here.

PUBLIC DEFENDER RECEPTIONIST
Beats me.

PAT
Well, can you or someone else here at least tell me what this says?

PUBLIC DEFENDER RECEPTIONIST
I certainly can't. I don't give legal advice. And our staff attorneys are far too busy to give free advice to just anybody, especially someone who can afford to pay for it himself.

PAT
But I can't. *[Pat looks at the two attorneys, who have been watching, but who now pointedly turn their backs on him. Nevertheless, he goes over to them.]* Excuse me. *[The attorneys do not speak, though they turn toward Pat.]* You're lawyers, aren't you. *[No response.]* Could you explain something to me?

ATTORNEY
Is this a legal question?

PAT
I guess so. It's about this summons. Can you tell me exactly what I'm charged with?

SECOND ATTORNEY
You want free legal advice?

PAT
Not advice, just --

ATTORNEY
Absolutely not.

[They turn away from him again. Pat backs away and heads for the door. The First Denizen makes a gesture to catch Pat's attention.]

FIRST DENIZEN
Hey, how is a lawyer like a rabbi.

[Long pause.]

PAT
I don't know.

PUBLIC DEFENDER RECEPTIONIST
They both study the law and the profits. Get it?

PAT
Uh, yeah. Very funny.

[Pat walks out. Lights down.]

Scene 7. Pat's and Sam's Home

[Lights up on the left half of the stage. Sam is sitting in a chair reading a magazine. Pat enters through the stage left door.]

SAM
Oh good, you're home. Long day at work?

PAT
I had my meeting today, so I had to work late. I bet you didn't even remember.

SAM
Of course I did. You went to the Public Defender's office. I just didn't know you'd be working late. How did it go.

PAT
It was a complete waste of time! My case was delayed three weeks for nothing. They won't represent me! I make too much money. I have a job! I'm no farther along than I was at the beginning.

SAM
Did you get a chance to ask --

PAT
No!

SAM
Well, don't take your frustrations out on me!

[Beat.]

PAT
You're right, I shouldn't take it out on you, but I'm angry.
The only person I got to talk to was the receptionist, and
even she cut me off. Then I tried to ask some attorneys who
were there, but they wouldn't give me the time of day. I hate
this! I can't do anything and I don't understand what's going
on! The whole system is screwed up! I feel like my feet are
caught in this huge meat-grinder and I'm being pulled in and
ground up, and when I yell for help, everybody turns away.

SAM
Well, when did you first step in the meat grinder, when you
were out –

PAT
No! Nothing happened!

SAM
How do you know!

[Beat.]

PAT
Because I'm not like that.

SAM
Like what.

PAT
Disorderly.

SAM
Violent and abusive.

[Pat clenches his fists.]

64

PAT
No!

SAM
I see. And when you've been drinking? We've had some pretty good fights.

PAT
Just verbal.

SAM
You raised your first once.

PAT
But I didn't hit you…

SAM
[Beat.] You know, I've left you alone about this. We haven't talked about it, because you don't remember, so there's nothing to talk about, but someday, maybe when you've been drinking again, it'll all come back to you, and maybe you'll decide it's time to tell me what happened and who you were with that night, and why you had blood on your sleeve.

PAT
It wasn't blood.

SAM
Well, it wasn't red wine.

PAT
How many times do I have to tell you, nothing happened.

[Sam makes a dismissive "okay" gesture.]

PAT
Just leave me alone for awhile.

SAM
With pleasure.

PAT
You wouldn't tell anybody I had blood on my sleeve, would
you?

[Sam just looks at him.]

SAM
I'll leave you alone for awhile.

[Pat exits to the bathroom. Lights down.]

Scene 8. The Courtroom

[Lights up on the right side of the stage, which is again the courtroom. The ADA is seated at a table in front. Other people, who may be the same or different, are seated around the room. The judge is seated on the bench. Pat is already in a seat, trying to stay awake.]

JUDGE
Omnium rerum quarum harum scarum. Non obstante veredicto, in flagrante delicto. Ave maria, pater noster, deus ex machina. *[Pat nods. His head drops as if asleep.]* I have been asked if the law favors the rich. It does not. The law is majestic in its equality. It forbids the rich as well as the poor from riding in freight cars, from begging in the streets, and from stealing bread. Taylor. Samuel Taylor. Scheduled for two-thirty. It is two-thirty-one by the courtroom clock. Non-appearance. Warrant. Barlow. Pat Barlow. *[Beat while Pat awakes with a start.]* Non --

PAT *[Stands.]*
Here, your honor.

JUDGE
Why didn't you respond when I called your name?

PAT
I was ... I was transfixed by the proceedings.

JUDGE
I can perhaps understand that. Where is your attorney.

PAT
I don't have one, your honor.

67

JUDGE
Don't you want an attorney? You have a right to one.

PAT
I ... I was here once before, your honor, and you told me to
go to the Public Defender's Office.

*[The First Denizen enters and sits down. One of the others
sidles over to him and whispers in his ear as the judge and
Pat continue to speak. He then becomes extremely agitated,
fidgety, and almost disruptive until he speaks.]*

JUDGE
Oh yes, I see that. That's exactly what I did. Did you do
that?

PAT
Yes, but they said I don't qualify for their services. I make
too much money.

[Everyone in the courtroom looks at Pat.]

JUDGE
You have a job?

PAT
Yes.

JUDGE
And you earn more than minimum wage?

PAT
Yes.

JUDGE

68

Well, if you make that kind of money, don't you want to hire
an attorney on your own?

PAT
I still don't think I can afford one.

JUDGE
But this is a criminal complaint. Do you realize that?

PAT
I get that much, your honor, but there's a lot about it I don't
understand.

JUDGE
What's not to understand? You could go to jail for up to
ninety days, and you could incur a fine of up to a thousand
dollars, which is more than most lawyers would charge for a
case like this -- well, a few lawyers, maybe not the most
competent ones. That's on the first charge, the disorderly
conduct. What don't you understand about that.

PAT
The first charge?!

JUDGE
Yes. On the second charge, resisting or obstructing, you
face a nine-month jail term and a ten thousand dollar fine.

PAT
The second charge?! Resisting or obstructing?!

JUDGE
Mr. Barlow. Are you ... under control, or are you suffering
from some ... malady.

PAT
I ... I don't understand what you're saying.

JUDGE
You have read the amended complaint, have you not?

PAT
The amended complaint?

JUDGE
The amended complaint, Mr. Barlow.

PAT
I ... No, I haven't. I haven't seen an amended complaint.

JUDGE
Well, if you didn't receive a complaint, why did you decide to come here today.

PAT
Your clerk gave me this date when I was here three weeks ago.

JUDGE
What brought you here that time.

PAT
This. The complaint.

JUDGE
What is the date on that.

PAT
July first.

JUDGE
There's the problem. The D.A.'s office filed this amended complaint on July second. You should have received a copy. That must have been an oversight by someone. *[To the ADA.]* Do you have an extra copy? *[The ADA gives it to Pat.]* Mr. Barlow, do you wish to stand mute or to consult an attorney.

PAT
Stand mute?

JUDGE
All right …

PAT
No, I mean what does stand mute mean.

JUDGE
I think I must even more strongly advise you to hire an attorney, and I'll grant you one more continuance to do so. Case adjourned, to be rescheduled in two months.

PAT
No!

JUDGE
What?!

PAT
Nothing. Your honor.

JUDGE
By the way, Mr. Barlow, a collection of cows is called a herd, and a group of geese is called a gaggle. Do you know what an accumulation of attorneys is called?

PAT
Uh ... no, your honor.

JUDGE
A quandary of lawyers.

[Long pause.]

PAT
Thank you, your honor.

FIRST DENIZEN
[Stands.] Excuse me, your honor.

JUDGE
What is it. Who are you.

FIRST DENIZEN
Samuel Taylor. Did you already call my case? My witnesses are waiting outside, and I was here on time. The clock in the hall said two-twenty-eight when I walked in.

JUDGE
I wouldn't know about that. You can't go by the clock in the hall. That clock there is the official time in this courtroom, and a warrant was ordered at two thirty-one.

FIRST DENIZEN
But I'm here, and my witnesses are here! Besides, the warrant hasn't been issued yet!

JUDGE
That is a detail. It was ordered. You may go to the sheriff's office and wait for it. If you can post a hundred dollars,

72

you'll be released and your case will be recalendared.

FIRST DENIZEN
No! No! No!

[The denizen screams and runs out.]

JUDGE
Clearly dangerous. Change bond to a thousand dollars.

[Blackout.]

[Curtain and intermission.]

ACT II
Scene 9. The Attorney's Office

[Lights up on the right half of the stage, which is now the attorney's office. The walls and horizontal spaces are covered with diplomas, certificates and other ostentatious wall
fillers. Prominently visible on the wall are the following: "A lawyer's time is his stock in trade. Abraham Lincoln",and "It is the trade of lawyers to question everything, yield nothing, and to talk by the hour. Thomas Jefferson". The attorney is seated at a large desk behind a pile of law books. Pat enters.]

PAT
Excuse me. I'm Pat Barlow. *[Pause.]* The receptionist said I should come in.

[The attorney motions for Pat to sit down, and he does. Long pause.]

ATTORNEY
Mr. Barlow.

PAT
Yes?

ATTORNEY
New client.

PAT
Yes ... maybe. Your ad said your initial consultation was free. I need to find out --

ATTORNEY
Criminal case?

PAT
Uh, yes, ma'am.

ATTORNEY
What are you accused of.

PAT
Well, the first complaint I got said disorderly conduct, but
when I was in court yesterday -- I can't believe it! They –
I'm sorry. Now there's an amended complaint, with a
second count, of something called resisting or obstructing.

ATTORNEY
Let me see. *[Pat hands a paper to the attorney.]* Branch
five, that's good. Judge Richmond and I are good friends.
[Pause.] It looks like a manageable case. Do you want me
to represent you?

PAT
Well, first, I'd like to understand it.

ATTORNEY
Why.

PAT
Why ... do I need to understand it?

ATTORNEY
Yes, I'm the one who has to understand it, not you.

PAT
But this is my case.

ATTORNEY
Well, of course, but I'm the attorney, and you're ... What
don't you understand.

PAT
I don't understand what's going on! These papers and court
proceedings make less sense all the time. The ground keeps
shifting under my feet.

ATTORNEY
Well, I can help you with that. But you do understand the
charges, don't you?

PAT
No! That's why I came to see you.

ATTORNEY
Well, it's D.C. and obstructing.

PAT
I know that much! I'm sorry. You see, I can't tell what that
is. What did I do? You lawyers have all this ... special
language. Resisting or obstructing. What does that mean.
Did I get in somebody's way? It sounds like a penalty in
football or something.

ATTORNEY
It can mean hindering, delaying, impeding, frustrating,
preventing, interfering, deceiving or misleading an officer.

PAT
Only an officer?

76

ATTORNEY
Yes.

PAT
So I did something to a cop?

ATTORNEY
That's what this says.

PAT
And D.C. What does that mean.

ATTORNEY
Violent, abusive –

PAT
I know that!

ATTORNEY
So what is it you don't understand.

PAT
Did I do all that or was I just singing too loud in my car.

ATTORNEY
Well, what did you do.

PAT
Nothing!

ATTORNEY
Ah, the innocent person defense. Very common, almost always unsuccessful, though we can leave it on the table for now. But if, for the sake of argument, and as you say, you really didn't do anything, what do you expect me to explain

to you.

PAT
[Defeated.] I don't know. *[Pause.]* All right, here's a question: if all those things are listed for D.C., does it mean I'm supposed to have done all of them?

ATTORNEY
Of course not, although saying "of course not" in answer to your question may perhaps be going a bit too far. The "or" in the sentence is a disjunctive conjunction, so you've been charged with any or all of the designated behavior. Behavior exceptionally under contrast with outstanding criminological bases of action. This is important because, although the burden of proof is on the State to prove you guilty beyond a reasonable doubt, the highest burden under the law, the State's task is actually made quite a bit easier because you can be found guilty of disorderly conduct if any of the aforementioned terms is proven. Evidence proffered in support of a limited term of the formulation is nevertheless admissible under all reformulations and for all configurations. In fact, D.C. is a really hard charge to beat if you've ever gone anywhere and done anything.

[Beat while Pat looks at the attorney quizzically.]

PAT
But can't I get off if the complaint's obviously wrong, for example, the date. If I didn't do anything on June seventh, the date it says in the complaint.

ATTORNEY
It's possible, if you have a strong alibi, such as being able to prove you were visiting the Pope at the time.

78

PAT
No, but the date's wrong.

ATTORNEY
What do you mean. You mean you did do something, and
they just got the date wrong?

PAT
They said it was at 2:45 A.M. on June seventh. If I did do
anything, it definitely wasn't then, it would've been the next
day, but I don't really remember.

ATTORNEY
Ah, the "I don't remember" defense. Still not a winner, but
getting better.

PAT
But the date, doesn't it mean anything?

ATTORNEY
Well --

PAT
Can they really just change the date to conform to ...
whatever it is?

ATTORNEY
Oh yes, yes, frequently they do.

PAT
So they hold all the cards.

ATTORNEY
Not at all.

PAT
What cards do I hold.

ATTORNEY
Well *[Beat.]* As a start, you're innocent until proven guilty.
And subsequently, the justice system is constrained under
the hypothetical definitions of adverse action. Perhaps it's
not really essential at this stage that you understand
everything. The point is, I do. I understand the charge and I
understand the legal system, and as I said, I know the judge
– You know the definition of the best lawyer in any
situation?

[Beat.]

PAT
Uh, no.

ATTORNEY
The one who knows both the law and the judge, and I would
be pleased to represent you.

PAT
Is that all the explanation you can give me?

ATTORNEY
I'm sure I could explain everything to you, but it may take
some time, and *[She points to the Lincoln quotation.]* as the
saying goes, time is money, and I don't actually represent
you yet.

PAT
How much would it cost me?

ATTORNEY
For defense of a misdemeanor, I'd have to charge you a
thousand dollar retainer to start, which will pay for up to
four hours of my time. If I settle it in less than that I still
keep the retainer. If it goes to a jury trial, it will undoubtedly
cost more than that, and you'll be charged on an hourly basis.

PAT
How can you do that.

ATTORNEY
Do what.

PAT
Charge a thousand dollars and keep all of it even if you don't
do the work.

ATTORNEY
Because you're paying for the accumulated expertise of three
years of law school and eighteen years of practice. Because
settling your case is worth that much. Because I have
overhead. Because lawyers make the rules.

PAT
I'm sorry. I can't afford it.

ATTORNEY
Oh well then, this initial consultation is over.

PAT
Well ...

ATTORNEY
Think it over. I'm sure you'll decide it's money well spent.

PAT
What did you say about a jury trial?

ATTORNEY
I said if it goes to a jury trial, it would cost much more.

PAT
I don't want to know how much, not now. But would I need
a jury trial?

ATTORNEY
Probably not. I should be able to settle this without a trial.

PAT
But it might go to trial?

ATTORNEY
Certainly, and if it does, you'll be in good hands with me.

PAT
But if I'm innocent, what difference does it make if you or
anyone else, uh, you know, does the ....

ATTORNEY
Tries the case?

PAT
Tries the case.

ATTORNEY
A not guilty verdict has nothing to do with the defendant's
innocence, and everything to do with the skill of the lawyer.
What do you think a jury is.

PAT
Uh, twelve people who decide whether a person is innocent
or guilty.

ATTORNEY
Not at all. A jury is twelve people who decide which side
has the better lawyer.

PAT
So you're saying if I can't afford to hire you ...?

[The attorney picks up the complaint and reads.]

ATTORNEY
Obstructing: imprisoned for up to nine months and a fine of
up to ten thousand dollars.

[Pat takes the complaint.]

PAT
I'll think about it. Thanks.

ATTORNEY
You're welcome. Come back any time. My door is always
open to my clients.

PAT
Good-bye.

ATTORNEY
Good-bye. Have a nice day.

[Pat exits. Lights down.]

Scene 10. Pat's and Sam's Home

[Lights up on the left half of the stage. Pat and Sam enter together from the kitchen.]

SAM
That was delicious. Why is it that even when you use my recipe, you manage to make a dish taste so much better than when I make it.

PAT
It's a well-known phenomenon. Having someone else do the cooking improves the flavor. I feel the same way whenever you steal one of my recipes.

SAM
When have I ever done that.

PAT
What.

SAM
Stolen one of your recipes.

PAT
Last Thanksgiving. My cherry pie.

SAM
Yours?

PAT
Of course. I got it from my grandmother. We always had cherry pie at Thanksgiving.

SAM

Your grandmother? I got it from _my_ grandmother.

PAT

You're crazy. My family always had cherry pie; that's where
I got the recipe. Your family always had pumpkin pie.

SAM

Who're you calling crazy. Let's look at the handwriting on
the cherry pie recipe. I know it'll be mine.

PAT

That won't prove anything. When you steal my recipes you
copy them over. And you make little changes. You use
different abbreviations for teaspoon and tablespoon.

SAM

I do not. What's the matter with you.

PAT

What's the matter with me? Nothing.

SAM

You were silent as a stone all through dinner, and now
you're trying to start an argument.

PAT

If I was quiet, I was just … I just … I guess I'm just upset.

SAM

About your case?

PAT

What else.

85

SAM
Did you go to see an attorney?

PAT
Yeah.

SAM
How much did it cost.

PAT
Nothing, yet.

SAM
How'd you choose one.

PAT
I looked in the Yellow Pages and found one near work that advertised a free initial consultation.

SAM
So what happened.

PAT
It was worse than worthless.

SAM
It didn't go well?

PAT
That's what I said.

SAM
Well, what does that mean.

PAT
How much money do we have in our savings account.

SAM
About fifteen hundred dollars. Why.

PAT
She wants a thousand just to take the case. And then I might
need more if it goes to trial. I told her that's too much. We
can't afford it.

SAM
You're right about that.

PAT
That's what I said.

SAM
And I said you're right about that.

PAT
Well, you don't have to beat it into the ground.

SAM
Who's beating things into the ground. You're the one who's
being obsessive. What's wrong with you.

PAT
You could be a little more supportive.

SAM
I'm agreeing with you! What do you want me to do.
[Pause.] Did you at least find out what the charges mean
and why there are two now?

PAT

I asked. She answered. I think. She never really answered me. Mostly all I can think about is the money. I told her I couldn't afford it, but since then I've been thinking. It does say I could actually go to jail, for up to nine months, and a ten thousand dollar fine, and if I don't do something to fight it, I might ... we might both end up losing a lot more than a thousand dollars. I feel like I have to afford it.

SAM

Whatever you say.

PAT

No, it isn't just whatever I say.

SAM

No, we'll do it for you, to get you out of whatever you got yourself into, which you still won't tell me about. Why don't you just tell me. It'd be easier for me to forgive you for something, anything, even infidelity, than to know that you don't trust me enough to tell me.

PAT

Don't you think I'd tell you if I knew anything?

[Long pause.]

SAM

I'm not sure about that.

PAT

What do you mean.

SAM

I mean I really don't know if I trust you to tell me. You

remember what happened in Chicago.

PAT
But I told you about that!

SAM
Later, much later.

PAT
A few days later.

SAM
Weeks. You didn't tell me for a long time. And maybe
we're in that period now before you decide to tell me. Once
a trust is violated, it's never the same. I truly don't know
whether I can trust you. *[Beat.]* Go on, hire an attorney.
Get yourself out of trouble with the law if you can. We'll
make do somehow. *[Beat.]* But stop stealing my recipes.

PAT
What?

SAM
Stealing recipes. That's where it starts! Go ahead; call your
mother. She'll tell you your grandmother never cooked a
cherry pie in her life. You never even had pie for
Thanksgiving. You always had beer. Twelve-packs. With a
blood chaser. Excuse me, I'm going to clean up.

[Sam exits through the kitchen door. Blackout.]

Scene 11. The Attorney's Office

[Lights up the right half of the stage, which is again the attorney's office. The attorney stands up at her desk as Pat enters.]

ATTORNEY
Good morning, Mr. Vincent. It's good to see you again. I've been thinking a lot about your case. I was sure you'd come back to ask me to work on it.

PAT
Who?

ATTORNEY
What?

PAT
Who did you say?

ATTORNEY
I don't think I understand.

PAT
When I walked in. You said "Good morning" and then you said someone's name. What name was that.

ATTORNEY
Yours, of course.

PAT
But what did you say.

ATTORNEY
Good morning, Mr. *[He looks down at the file.]* Barlow. Oh,

I misspoke before. I'm sorry. I has just finished a long
interview with Mr. Vincent.

PAT
I didn't see anyone leave, and I've been waiting for half an
hour.

ATTORNEY
He left just before that, and I've been working on his file
since then. A very sad case. I may have difficulty helping
him. He put off retaining me until it was almost too late.

PAT
All right. I get the point. So what have you been thinking
about.

ATTORNEY
What?

PAT
The other thing you said when I came in was that you'd been
thinking a lot about my case. So what have you been
thinking about, or was it really Mr. Vincent's case you were
thinking about.

ATTORNEY
Oh, just the number of factual and legal issues it raises, and
the need for some in-depth investigation and legal research if
we're to prevail.

PAT
But tell me something specific: [Beat.] tell me what I have
to prove.

ATTORNEY
Oh, you don't have to prove anything. That's the beauty of criminal defense work. The state has the burden of proof, and all we have to do is poke holes in their case.

PAT
I wish you wouldn't use that word.

ATTORNEY
"Holes"? "Poke"?

PAT
No, "criminal". I'm not, am I?

ATTORNEY
Not yet. I mean you're innocent until proven guilty.

PAT
Could you say "unless" instead of "until"?

ATTORNEY
That's just the standard phrase: "innocent until proven guilty".

PAT
"Until" sounds like it's just a matter of time. Couldn't it be "innocent unless proven guilty"?

ATTORNEY
Well, of course, you're innocent in the law's eyes unless you're convicted.

PAT
Why don't I feel better? Something about it still sounds inevitable. I'm beginning to think it's "innocent until

arrested", and then suddenly everybody considers you guilty.
I tell you what, can you just show me the law?

ATTORNEY
What?

PAT
Show me the law. It must exist somewhere. In a book?

ATTORNEY
Are you serious?

PAT
Sure. Can you show me that?

ATTORNEY
You want to look at the statutes? They're really
incomprehensible to ordinary mortals.

PAT
Maybe so, but I want to see.

[The attorney looks for the right book.]

ATTORNEY
Statutes, they must be around here somewhere. ... I know I
used them last month. ... They won't do you any good,
anyway. ... Aha, here they are. *[She unearths a volume,
whose pages creak as she opens it.]* Here, volume 5, chapter
947, section oh-one. Disorderly conduct.

PAT
It's there. You're right! I'm impressed. So all those numbers
and squiggles really do mean something. Are these statute
books in the public library?

ATTORNEY
Well yes, but I wouldn't advise you to try to research the law
on your own. It's very dangerous.

PAT
Why.

ATTORNEY
Well, you see, the law's not all in one place. You have to
look at the statutes and then at the cases and then at the holy,
I mean the authoritative, commentaries.

PAT
What is this.

ATTORNEY
Are you reading the statute book?

PAT
Yes. The very next entry after my statute says "defendant
was properly convicted of disorderly conduct where he
appeared on a stage wearing a minimum of clothing
intending to and succeeding in causing a loud reaction in the
audience". What is that.

ATTORNEY
That's a case.

PAT
I'll say.

ATTORNEY
Such cases help define the law.

PAT
So some fellow was found guilty of disorderly conduct for
prancing around on a stage in his underwear?

ATTORNEY
I wouldn't know without reading the case.

PAT
Are cases in some other book?

ATTORNEY
I have no intention of telling you how to do legal research.
It's far more difficult than you think.

PAT
Okay.

ATTORNEY
Okay?

PAT
Okay.

ATTORNEY
Okay? As in "Yes, I want you to be my attorney"?

PAT
Yes.

[The attorney's face lights up, but he stifles it.]

ATTORNEY
I'm pleased to hear that ... because now I'll be able to help
you. Do you have the retainer?

95

PAT
Yes.

[Same stifled reflex.]

ATTORNEY
Then we're all set. *[She picks up the phone and pushes two buttons]* Terry, will you prepare a retainer agreement, please. A thousand dollars. Uh ... *[She looks at the file.]* Pat Barlow. My secretary will take care of the details, since the money isn't important to me. I'll get the police reports to see what their evidence is and who their witnesses are, and I'll get in touch with you when I have a better grasp of things. Don't worry. I'm your attorney now. Just show up when I tell you to.

PAT
All right. Thanks.

[They shake hands and Pat exits. The attorney does a jig or other celebratory movement. After a moment, the attorney picks up the phone and punches two numbers.]

ATTORNEY
Is he gone? Did he sign it? Did he pay? Yeah!! Close the office, break out that bottle of old scotch, and we'll take the rest of the day off.

[Lights down.]

Scene 12. Pat's and Sam's Home

[Lights up on the left half of the stage. Sam is sitting and reading a magazine, with a half-full highball glass by her side. She is dressed seductively, and it becomes evident that she's been drinking, but not too much. Pat enters through the front door with an armload of books.]

SAM
Well, hello. *[She gets up and greets him with a hug and a kiss.]* I thought we agreed to spend the evening together after you talked to this lawyer. See, I remember your meetings and what you do. We might was well celebrate the expenditure of a thousand dollars for a good cause. Now tell me why you've kept me waiting and where you've been and what are all those books.

PAT
They're law books. The statutes and some cases. There's a case about indecent exposure.

SAM
Is that what you did?! Well, I want to hear all the details, or maybe we should re-enact it.

PAT
No! It's just the first case I found under disorderly conduct.

SAM
Oh. Well then, let's not talk about that. Come on, put those things down and have a drink with me. Have a couple of drinks, to catch up. I'll get you one.

[Sam starts for the kitchen door.]

97

PAT
I can't.

SAM
You can't?! You agreed we'd spend the evening alone
together and talk.

PAT
I know, but when I talked to the lawyer today I found out
about these, so I went to the library, and I've got to get to
work on them.

*[Long pause as he puts them down, stacks them up, and sits
down with one.]*

SAM
You're serious. This is how you intend to spend your
evening?

PAT
Sam, I've got to. We just spent a thousand dollars. This is
more important than ... sitting and getting drunk.

SAM
And talking.

PAT
And talking.

SAM
And spending time together.

PAT
Yes.

[She takes his hand and puts it on her breast.]

SAM
So all this is more important than I am?

PAT
Well, no, but ...

[Pause.]

SAM
It obviously is. *[She drops his hand.]* If there was any chance for us to communicate about this, this was it. You might just remember why you're in this mess, or you might just decide it's time to tell me what you know, and we could clear the air. You know, two people don't keep a relationship going just because they've made some promise to each other, it's the promise that continues if both people keep working at it.

PAT
Well, you sure didn't like it when I told you the last time.

SAM
No, I damn well didn't. Should I have liked it?! You wanted me to forgive and forget as soon as you told me. Well, it isn't that easy. I couldn't do that until a few days later, but I did, because nothing's more important than telling the truth. I admit, honesty can have painful consequences, but in the long run, honesty's more important than anything else, even fidelity. Pat, I'm afraid you're becoming obsessed with this.

PAT
You think I shouldn't be!? Every bit of this I can make sense

of could be the difference between freedom and jail.

SAM
Okay, forget it. Do your legal research. But as far as I'm concerned, you just missed your chance. All your appeals have been used up.

[Sam starts toward the door, then stops and retrieves her glass before exiting. Lights down.]

Scene 13. The Courtroom`

[Lights up on the right half of the stage, which is again the courtroom. The judge is seated on the bench. Pat enters and sits next to the First Denizen. The Second Attorney is questioning the Second Denizen, who is in the witness chair.]

FIRST DENIZEN
Hi.

PAT
Hello.

FIRST DENIZEN
Say, do you know the difference between a lawyer and a boxing referee?

PAT
Uh no. What's the difference.

DENIZEN
A boxing referee doesn't get paid more for a longer fight.

PAT
Very funny. What's going on.

FIRST DENIZEN
Sh.

JUDGE
Meenin **ayee**tha **thee**a peeleeadeeo **akill**eeos. You may continue your questioning.

101

SECOND ATTORNEY
You were driving your vehicle within the speed limit east on
Allen Boulevard, weren't you?

SECOND DENIZEN
Yes.

SECOND ATTORNEY
And how far away was the truck when you first noticed it.

SECOND DENIZEN
About half a block away.

SECOND ATTORNEY
And how far away was the truck when it struck your car.

[Pause.]

SECOND DENIZEN
Uh …

JUDGE
Next question.

SECOND ATTORNEY
But the witness didn't answer the question

JUDGE
Move on.

SECOND ATTORNEY
I object. You're favoring the other side, and you're
preventing me from obtaining necessary information. The
answer to that question is essential to my case.

102

JUDGE
Then rephrase the question.

SECOND ATTORNEY
Rephrase it? What do you mean.

JUDGE
The question you asked was absurd. You may ask another.

SECOND ATTORNEY
Well then, how far away from your car was the truck when it struck it.

JUDGE
Even worse. Now the syntax as well as the meaning is muddled. Try again. No, never mind. *[To the witness.]* Did the truck and your car collide?

SECOND DENIZEN
Yes, your honor.

JUDGE
[To the attorney.] You may proceed.

SECOND ATTORNEY
Do you intend to do all my questioning?

JUDGE
Not if you can do it yourself.

[Pause.]

SECOND ATTORNEY
You were in the car with your brother, weren't you?

SECOND DENIZEN
Yes.

SECOND ATTORNEY
And one of you was killed in the accident, isn't that true?

SECOND DENIZEN
Yes.

SECOND ATTORNEY
Which one of you was killed.

[Beat. The judge looks pained.]

SECOND DENIZEN
My brother.

SECOND ATTORNEY
Shortly after the accident, the police arrived, didn't they.

SECOND DENIZEN
Yes.

SECOND ATTORNEY
And was your brother still dead when the police arrived?

JUDGE
Next question.

SECOND ATTORNEY
Your honor, if it please the court --

JUDGE
It does not. Pleasure has long been out of the question.
Perhaps a momentary pause would be beneficial, to collect

104

our overtaxed wits.

SECOND ATTORNEY
Thank you, your honor. Actually, I was about to ask for a slightly longer break. I believe that the doctrine of res ipsa loquitur as enunciated by the Court of Appeals en banc in Village of Wapping Falls versus Consolidated Papers, three-fifty-nine eff supp seventy-four, 1954, would require a ruling that counsel is to be allowed time liberally to visit the little girls' room.

JUDGE
Motion granted. We'll take this matter up again when counsel is finished with her pottie break. *[To the Second Denizen.]* You may stand down. *[The Second Denizen looks at the judge quizzically.]* You may leave the witness stand and return to your chair. *[She then gets up from the witness chair and sits elsewhere.]* Why don't we take a brief recess. *[The judge shuffles papers.]*

FIRST DENIZEN
I thought you weren't coming back.

PAT
I thought you were in jail.

FIRST DENIZEN
Oh yeah, the last time I saw you. I was in for eight days until my family could raise a thousand dollars, and I lost my job because of it, but I'm back again today. Another status call. They just want to see if I'll show up, or if they can get me for bail-jumping. What're you here for, anyway?

PAT
My attorney sent me a letter to show up for a plea today, not

even to meet him ahead of time, just to be here at the scheduled time. No discussions, no client consultation, no nothing. I don't know what's going on!

FIRST DENIZEN
But what charges are you here for.

PAT
Disorderly conduct and resisting or obstructing. Do you know what those are?

FIRST DENIZEN
Sure, D.C.'s anything that can be done in public or in private, and resisting or obstructing is anything that can be done to an officer. Usually, though, it's what they use for lying to an officer.

PAT
Lying to an officer? *[Beat.]* Oh. Or maybe ... would they use that for ... hiding or destroying evidence?

FIRST DENIZEN
Yeah. Say, did you hear the one about the doctor, the engineer, and the lawyer at their best friend's funeral?

PAT
Uh ...

DENIZEN
Well, they and their friend had agreed that they each wanted to "take it with them" when they went, and that they would each give a hundred dollars to whoever departed before they did. So at the funeral, the doctor went up to the casket and slipped a hundred-dollar bill under the deceased's folded hands. Then the engineer went up and put a gold coin worth

a hundred dollars into the deceased's hand. The lawyer went last, and she went up to the casket, took the hundred-dollar bill and the gold coin, and left a check for three hundred dollars. *[Beat.]* Do you get it.

PAT
I got it, and I'm beginning to understand the charm of lawyer jokes.

[The attorney enters and sits next to Pat. The denizen moves away.]

PAT
I don't know what you expect me to do, but I'm not pleading.

ATTORNEY
Of course you are. That's what we're here for.

PAT
But how can I say I'm guilty when I don't agree with it or even really understand it! I absolutely refuse.

ATTORNEY
Guilty, of course not. You enter a plea of not guilty.

PAT
Not guilty? Is that what pleading means?

ATTORNEY
Of course, at this stage. Guilty pleas come later in the process. No-one's entered a plea of guilty at an initial appearance since 1986 when Crazy Mary Mahoney tried to enter a plea of guilty to shoplifting.

[Beat.]

PAT
What happened.

ATTORNEY
The court found her mentally incompetent, as proven by her behavior in entering a
plea of guilty. As far as I know, she's still in Mendota *[the name of a local mental health center]* for evaluation.

PAT
Well, how can I even say "not guilty" if I don't really know what happened.

ATTORNEY
Don't be absurd. That's what "not guilty" means. It means "I'm not guilty, or I don't know if I'm guilty, or even if I'm guilty, you're gonna have to prove it".

PAT
Oh.

JUDGE
Well, it doesn't look like she's coming back any time soon. What do we have that we can squeeze in. Here's a quickie. State versus Pat Barlow. Continued initial appearance.

[The ADA moves to the front table. The attorney and Pat stand.]

ATTORNEY
Your honor, Mr. Barlow appears in person, and by attorney Jene Smith of Smith, Stein, Sharif and Sugimoto, S.C.

JUDGE
Do you have a copy of the amended complaint and waive the reading?

ATTORNEY
Yes, your honor.

JUDGE
How does Mr. Barlow plead to the charge, Ms. Smith.

ATTORNEY
Not guilty.

JUDGE
The case will be scheduled for a pretrial conference. You can expect to return in about six weeks. Case adjourned. *[The ADA leaves the table. The Second Attorney re-enters and returns to the table.]* Ah, just in time. That must just have been a number two. Now where did I put your file. *[To the Second Denizen.]* You may return to the stand and you are still under oath, do you understand?

SECOND DENIZEN
Yes, your honor.

JUDGE
You may return to the fray.

SECOND ATTORNEY
Let me try another tack. *[She hands a photo to the Second Denizen.]* The photo you have there shows your car before the accident, doesn't it?

SECOND DENIZEN
Yes. That's me standing next to my car.

109

SECOND ATTORNEY
And were you present when that picture was taken?

JUDGE
That's enough. We need a sidebar. Please approach the bench.

[The Second Attorney approaches the bench.]

PAT
[Sotto voce.] Do you mean after months of delays, all the system wanted was to hear me say I'm not guilty? And it didn't even want to hear it from me! Why did I have to spend half my day here in court on top of all the other time I've spent here. Couldn't you have done it for me?

ATTORNEY
Absolutely not. This is a criminal matter. You have to appear in person. If you could just have an attorney make your plea for you in such a serious matter, it might cause defendants to lose their respect for the solemnity of our system of justice.

PAT
Lose their respect for the solemnity of our system of justice?!

[Pat storms out. Blackout.].

Scene 14. The District Attorney's Office

[Lights up on the left half of the stage, which is now the office of an assistant district attorney, cluttered with files. The walls are covered with travel posters to not very exotic places, such as Atlanta or Denver. Pat and the attorney enter together.]

PAT
Will you tell me what we're doing here?

ATTORNEY
We'll see what the D.A. wants out of this case. It's possible we can get you off on a reduced charge.

PAT
Can you explain something to me first?

ATTORNEY
What.

PAT *[pulls out a paper]*
I ran across a reference to disorderly conduct in Corpus Juris Secundum –

ATTORNEY
Are you really reading CJS?

PAT
Yes.

ATTORNEY
Do you understand it?

PAT
Not much. That's why I asked you to explain something.

ATTORNEY
I do not approve. That is not going to help.

PAT
But I need to understand some of this stuff. What does this mean: "The offense of disorderly conduct is of common-law origin, but in several jurisdictions it is a statutory crime."

ATTORNEY
I'd have to give you a course in Anglo-American legal history. It would take too long.

PAT
Well then, how about "The offense of disorderly conduct may therefore be committed in ways other than those specified in the statute." Is that true?

ATTORNEY
Sure.

PAT
Like what.

ATTORNEY
That's what all those cases are about.

PAT
Are you serious?

[The A.D.A. stands up from behind one of the stacks of files.]

112

ASSISTANT DISTRICT ATTORNEY
Hi, Jene. You're back. How was the trip to Jamaica?

ATTORNEY
Fantastic. It's trips like that that make the daily grind worth
while. I was just talking to my travel agent this morning and
I'm looking at an African safari next fall.

ASSISTANT DISTRICT ATTORNEY
Man, I wish I could afford Jamaica.

ATTORNEY
It's not that hard to do if you keep your priorities straight. I
mean, what's more important, a new car every couple of
years or some regular R and R, especially to a place with
liberated views on drug use.

ASSISTANT DISTRICT ATTORNEY
Well neither, actually.

ATTORNEY
Aw come on. My travel agent could put together a first-
class Jamaica package for the retainer on one case.

ASSISTANT DISTRICT ATTORNEY
We don't work the way you do. You know that. The clients
who walk in your door are meal tickets, or airline tickets.
Each file I get just means more work for the same pay. *[The
attorney hands the A.D.A. a business card.]*

ATTORNEY
Here, Diane, at Olympus Travel. Give her a call. I'm a
good customer. Tell her I sent you and besides getting the
best service in town, I'll get a referral rebate off my next trip.

ASSISTANT DISTRICT ATTORNEY
Right. I'll ask her about tour packages to Cleveland. What's the case.

ATTORNEY
Barlow, Pat Barlow. Just D.C. and obstructing. What do you want on it.

[The A.D.A. looks for and with some difficulty finds the file.]

ASSISTANT DISTRICT ATTORNEY
Barlow. I remember that name. Oh yeah, strange case. No priors, not so much as a speeding ticket. *[The A.D.A. looks at Pat for the only time during this scene.]*

ATTORNEY
That right? Then why not just dismiss it, or reduce it to an ordinance violation. Get some money out of him and call it even.

ASSISTANT DISTRICT ATTORNEY
Can't do it if there are three separate charges.

ATTORNEY
Okay, so what's the problem. There are only two.

ASSISTANT DISTRICT ATTORNEY
Not any more. I just got done dictating a new charge of bail-jumping.

PAT
Bail-jumping?!

[Both attorneys reacts as if Pat had screamed in a library, shushing him and telling him to be quiet.]

114

ATTORNEY
You don't say a thing!

PAT
But I didn't jump bail. I'm here!

ASSISTANT DISTRICT ATTORNEY
Mr. Barlow!

ATTORNEY
You don't say anything. I'll explain it to you later.

ASSISTANT DISTRICT ATTORNEY
He failed to show up for a status conference a couple of
weeks ago. Were you his attorney then?

ATTORNEY
A couple of weeks ago? Yeah. I didn't get notice of any
status conference, or if I did, I sent it right to him. Did you
get notice of a status conference?

PAT
No! Bail-jumping?

ATTORNEY
You can't issue a bail-jumping charge if we never received
notice.

ASSISTANT DISTRICT ATTORNEY
Sorry. We have proof in the file it was mailed to you, and if
the U.S. Postal Service doesn't deliver it, that's your
problem, not ours.

ATTORNEY
We never got it.

ASSISTANT DISTRICT ATTORNEY
The legal presumption is you did, and the burden's on you to
prove otherwise. So that adds another nine months jail and
ten thousand dollars. Since it's three separate offenses on
three separate occasions, no dismissals or ordinance
violations, and no first offenders. We'll need some jail on
this, at least sixty days. No fine, just court costs. Oh, and by
the way, I probably shouldn't tell you this, tell you my
strategy, but I don't have time to play games. Look at all
these cases. I've decided not to proceed with the D.C. Too
much trouble. The witnesses are unreliable and probably
unlocatable. I can prove the other two with just officers and
court documents. Talk it over and get back to me. I gotta
get back to work.

*[The A.D.A. vanishes behind a pile of paper. The attorney
and Pat turn and walk to a far corner of the room, where
they converse in lowered voices.]*

ATTORNEY
Don't forget to call my travel agent! You heard what she
said. Sixty days on three misdemeanors isn't a bad offer.

PAT
Are you just rolling over and accepting that? What about
this bail-jumping thing!! I think it stinks. Why should I go
to jail for something I didn't do, and something else they just
cooked up out of thin air. And what's this about not
proceeding with the D.C.?! Does that mean she's going to
dismiss it?

116

ATTORNEY
Uh huh.

PAT
Can they do that?

ATTORNEY
Just drop it?

PAT
Yeah.

ATTORNEY
Do you object to dismissing one of the counts?

PAT
Yes! That's what caused all this trouble. I've gotta find out
about it! If they try to dismiss it, can we insist on a trial on it
anyway?

ATTORNEY
That's not the way it works. Now don't be stupid about this.
You don't object when the D.A. offers to dismiss one out of
three counts.

PAT
But don't I get to prove I'm innocent, or at least find out
what happened?

ATTORNEY
No, that's not the way it works.

*[A sign appears somewhere that says "That's not the way it
works."]*

117

PAT
How about the other charges. If the D.C. goes away, don't the other two go away, too?

ATTORNEY   PAT *[almost simultaneously]*
That's not the way   ... not the way it works!
it works.

ATTORNEY
Well, do you want to take the offer or not.

PAT
Just like that?! No! Are you really serious?

ATTORNEY
Yeah. That's the way it works.

[A sign appears somewhere that says "That's the way it works."]

PAT
At least give me some time to think about it. I may still want a trial.

ATTORNEY
Well, it's your choice. A trial can be expensive, and we may not even be able to get on the calendar this year.

PAT
Not this year?!

ATTORNEY
Listen, I don't have much time right now. I'm already late for calendar call in branch three. Give me a call in my office tomorrow afternoon. Okay?

[The attorney starts moving toward the door of the office. Pat holds back. Very slowly they move to the door.]

PAT
That doesn't work. When I call you, you're never there, and you never call back. Are you sure you'll be there tomorrow?

ATTORNEY
Sure. We'll talk about it tomorrow.

[They exit. Lights down.]

Scene 15. Pat's and Sam's Home

[Sam is sitting in a tight spotlight on the only uncluttered spot on the floor, surrounded by piles of books and papers, figuring with a pen on a pad of paper. She jumps up when Pat enters. He is carrying more books, which he puts down on the spot where Sam was sitting.]

SAM
Oh, I'm so glad you're home. I was hoping you'd be here soon, 'cause I need to tell somebody, and I want you to be the first, to hear about ... ta da!, my promotion and raise. Starting in two weeks, I'll be manager of all parcel delivery services in the metropolitan area.

PAT
Congratulations.

SAM
And I'll be making another three thousand dollars a year.

PAT
That's good. That'll help.

SAM
You heard what I said?

PAT
Yeah, another three thousand a year.

SAM
Well, you don't need to dance around and make a big fuss about it.

PAT
No, that's great. I'm pleased. Congratulations.

SAM
Don't I even get a hug and a kiss?

PAT
Oh. Sure.

SAM
Never mind. I don't think I want it now.

PAT
Oh, come on.

SAM
What are you researching now, obsessions?

PAT
Very funny. You think what I'm doing now is an obsession?

SAM
Well, you're beginning to ignore everything else, like your wife's announcement that she just got a promotion.

PAT
I did not ignore it. I congratulated you.

SAM
Whoopee. If you're not obsessed now, I'd hate to see you when you are.

PAT
I am not obsessed!

SAM

You are! *[Pause.]* Breathe. Calm. So what happened today.

PAT

She said to call her this afternoon and we'd talk. I didn't call. I left work early and went to her office at one-thirty. The receptionist said she was at lunch but she'd be back soon. I waited until five, with the receptionist saying she expected her back any minute. Do you think she showed up? Not on your life! What do they do.

SAM

Maybe she was stuck in a trial.

PAT

Don't make up excuses for her! I don't need you on her side, too! Her travel agent probably called at noon with a great thousand dollar package to Rio.

SAM

Whatever you say.

PAT

And then when I stopped off at work on the way home, there was a message from the attorney's secretary saying I'm supposed to show up at the District Attorney's office next week. No explanation. Just show up. I just know I'm about to be sold down the river.

SAM

Why don't you call the attorney and ask what it's about.

PAT

Ha! Don't make me laugh. I've called before, and she's

never returned one of my calls!

SAM
Why don't you fire her and hire somebody else.

PAT
Because she's got my money and won't give it back, even if she's done nothing, and why should I think the next one'd be any better. She's getting paid to keep me in the dark.

SAM
Can she do that?

PAT
That's what she says.

SAM
That's a racket.

PAT
She said lawyers make the rules.

SAM
So what happens now.

PAT
She obviously wants to reach an agreement where I plead guilty to something so this'll all go away and everybody can be happy except me. And then she can keep the rest of my money without working for it. *[Beat.]* It's a good thing she never actually did any work on my disorderly conduct charge, because that's gone now. *[Pause.]* And all the time I spent trying to understand it!

123

SAM

The disorderly conduct charge is gone?! Why.

PAT

The D.A. said something about witness problems and it being too much trouble.

SAM

Witness problems. What happened.

PAT

I don't know. I wish I had a clue. And I can't ask my lawyer, 'cause that was all the district attorney said, and I can't ask the district attorney, 'cause she can't talk to me without my lawyer present.

SAM

What was the offer again?

PAT

The offer for me to go to jail?

SAM

If you want to call it that, yeah.

PAT

Sixty days in jail. At least I think that's what she said. I'm never sure whether what I hear is what they say. Nothing means what it seems to mean. It's as if they have their own language, their own secret code.

SAM

No fine?

PAT
No. I remember that. She said just court costs.

SAM
Like five hundred dollars?

PAT
I don't know.

SAM
Well, that wouldn't be too bad.

PAT
On top of the thousand I already tossed down that rabbit hole?!

SAM
We could afford that.

PAT
Are you saying I should just give in, let 'em give me a criminal record and send me to jail for something I didn't do, as long as we can afford it?

SAM
I didn't say that.

PAT
You said "That wouldn't be too bad."

SAM
I was just saying it wouldn't be too bad if the court costs were five hundred dollars. Listen, I don't want this to happen to you, and I worry about you.

PAT
You do?

SAM
Of course.

PAT
That's good to hear.

SAM
I don't like seeing you like this.

PAT
What would you think if I went to jail.

[Beat.]

SAM
Well ...

PAT
Have you thought about it?

SAM
Yes.

PAT
Well?

SAM
I've thought about it, as a possibility. [Beat.] And if it does
happen, it isn't the end of the world. Lots of people have
brushes with the law, and they just go on with their lives.

PAT

But I'm on my way to becoming a convicted criminal! I feel so helpless, like I'm walking down an empty road and I hear a truck rumbling toward me. I turn around to look and I see it, but it won't stop, and I run, but for some reason I can't get out of its way. *[Sam stands and hugs Pat.]* And you're on the side of the road watching me and you don't even care if I get run over.

SAM

That's not true. I do care, but what can I do, and what real difference will a conviction make. Maybe it'll be good to get it over with. A conviction won't change anything between you and me. Look, can you try to forget your case, just tonight, for my sake? I want to go out and celebrate.

PAT

I may go to jail, and you want to celebrate?!

SAM

Well, how about celebrating my promotion and raise, which will help us a lot if you have to pay a fine or if you're ... unable to work for awhile.

PAT

You're planning on my getting convicted, aren't you!

SAM

I'm not planning on it, but yes, I'm planning for it. You admit you're not sure what's going to happen and ... I've got to plan. You haven't been paying much attention to things like the apartment or the finances these days.

PAT

How can I! I feel sick to my stomach whenever I let myself

think about what's happening, which is most of the time. I
even dream about courts and attorneys' offices.

SAM
Come on, let's do something to forget it.

PAT
Like what.

SAM
I don't know. How about going out for a movie or a show.
We haven't done that in a long time. Or how about Robin's
apartment-warming party. That's tonight, remember.

PAT
I'm supposed to go to an apartment-warming party for one of
your friends and pretend to have fun?

SAM
Robin is both of our friends, and basically, yes. Life goes
on, you know. And who knows, if you could act like you're
having fun, maybe you'd lighten up a little.

PAT
I'm afraid if I'm surrounded by happy people, especially
people who've been drinking, I'll get even more depressed,
probably maudlin.

SAM
Well yes, you might, but maybe not, maybe you'll forget
your problem.

PAT
My problem! Is that what it is!

SAM
No, no. Just forget it.

PAT
Why don't you just go on to the party without me.

SAM
I don't want to do that.

PAT
Well, somebody should go, right? I agree with you on that.
But I don't want to. Go by yourself. Tell them I'm sick and I
don't want to infect anybody else. It's pretty close to the
truth. Go on.

SAM
Are you sure?

PAT
Yeah, go on. I wouldn't be good company.

SAM
Well, I guess ... Will you be okay?

PAT
Yeah. I'll be okay.

SAM
I won't stay long.

PAT
No, stay as long as you want. I really wish you would. I'd
only feel guilty if you decided to leave early because of me.
Why did I use that word. I hate it!

SAM
What word.

PAT
Guilty! You think I'm guilty, too.

SAM
Pat, if I feel any differently toward you, it's because of what
you did that night, and how you've acted since, not anything
the courts or the police do.

PAT
But I didn't do anything that night.

SAM
Listen, I don't want to start anything, but I think you should
understand. Do you know why I'm so sure you're not telling
me everything?

PAT
Why.

SAM
Because you're so sure you won't ever remember anything.
If it were just a blank memory, you'd think it might come
back someday. Would you believe me if I stayed out all
night, came home at 6:30 in the morning, with blood all over
me from god-knows-what brawl, and claimed I couldn't
remember anything past two a.m., and I was sure I wouldn't
ever remember anything?

PAT
I did not have blood all over me. It was just a little bit on my
sleeve, if it was even blood, and we don't know that for sure.
And I told you about drinking in the parking lot after bar

time. Don't exaggerate.

SAM
Don't exaggerate! Those are just details! Just tell me the
truth. I can handle it. I've handled things before. You
should trust me, and trust our relationship. If you don't think
you can trust it, then neither can I. I can handle it a damn
sight better than thinking you're lying to me and covering up
whatever it is you did.

PAT
You wouldn't tell the police there was blood all over me,
would you?

[This is the point at which she gives up.]

SAM
Why not! Why the hell not! Somebody's got to tell the
truth. You sure as hell can't! And if you really really don't
remember, how the hell can you be so sure the cops aren't
right.

PAT
You believe the cops?

SAM
I didn't say that, but *[Beat.]* why not. Why the hell not! If
they say you did something, and if you were drunk and don't
remember .... Who were you with that night.

PAT
Nobody!

SAM
Of course not. Just like you weren't with that sales rep in

131

Chicago, until you decided to tell me about it the next time we had a few drinks together. You know, up until then I believed that sex was something special between us. When that went, I had to believe that there was still a special relationship between us, and honesty was a big part of that. But if that's not there, why should we stay together. Can you tell me why we should stay together?

[Pause.]

PAT
Because I love you.

SAM
What does that mean.

PAT
What do you mean, what does that mean.

SAM
Does that mean anything. Those words, that word means nothing, because it means anything.

PAT
I need you.

SAM
For what.

PAT
What do I need you for?

SAM
Yes.

PAT
For … for me.

SAM
Pat, I don't need poetry or the right words, though they help,
if you could just show it.

PAT
Show what.

SAM
That love isn't just for you. *[Beat.]* You don't get it, do you.
Okay, forget it. Let's go back to the main issue here. Was it
somebody from your work? Somebody I know? Did you
make up that whole drunken bullshit story just to cover up
having sex with somebody?

PAT
No!

SAM
Yeah, right. I wish I could be sure, but once trust is broken
…. I want a list of everyone at your work, everybody who
was at the party, and where they live.

PAT
Oh, come off it.

SAM
Don't "come off it" with me! You owe me for making me
worry all night!

PAT
What if I don't know everybody at the party.

SAM

I don't really need a list. All I'm really looking for is one
name.

PAT

I can't believe this. My own wife!

SAM

Pat, what do you expect. You give me a cock-and-bull story,
nine parts beer and 2 parts cover-up, about not remembering
who you spent the night with, and on top of it you go out and
–

[Pat grabs Sam by the shoulders and shakes her.]

PAT

Just shut the fuck up!!

*[Sam glares at Pat with a mixture of fear, anger and
amazement.]*

PAT

Sorry! That didn't happen!

*[Pat turns and runs out the front door, slamming it behind
him.]*

Scene 16. The District Attorney's Office

[Lights up on the left half of the stage, which is still the A.D.A.'s office. The attorney and the ADA are talking.]

ASSISTANT DISTRICT ATTORNEY
God, I'd just be happy with the one-day layover in San Francisco. Did you take a cablecar to Fisherman's Wharf?

ATTORNEY
Been there. Done that.

ASSISTANT DISTRICT ATTORNEY
Did you eat in Chinatown?

ATTORNEY
Been there, too many times. I spent the entire evening at a great little restaurant on ... *[Pat enters.]* Oh, Jerry. Good. Listen, I just need to talk to you for a second. *[He stands and leads Pat to a corner of the room, where they converse again in lowered voices.]* Here's the deal: I know you're worried about the jail. I think we can knock the sixty days in half to thirty if you agree to a thousand dollar fine. What do you say? *[Pat shakes his head, partly in disbelief.]* I can see you're still not happy. Well then, we can threaten to take it to trial -- of course you'd have to pay for it -- but maybe I can get it down farther. I'll offer thirty days plus the fine. Okay? *[Pat stares as if poleaxed. The attorney turns and starts walking back.]* Okay, we're ready. *[He sits and motions Pat to sit.]* No deal. I really think you're going to have proof problems with this case. We're ready to take it to trial, and I think Jerry'll be a good witness.

ASSISTANT DISTRICT ATTORNEY
Who?

135

ATTORNEY
Jerry here.

ASSISTANT DISTRICT ATTORNEY
Don't you mean Pat?

[The attorney starts to open his briefcase, realizes it would take too much time.]

ATTORNEY
Is your name Pat?

[Pat nods.]

ATTORNEY
Put him, whatever his name is, on the stand. He'll be a good witness.

ASSISTANT DISTRICT ATTORNEY
Oh.

ATTORNEY
The jury'll like him, sympathize with him. You'll waste half a day and you won't get a conviction.

ASSISTANT DISTRICT ATTORNEY
Yes I will. I can do it standing on my head, and you know it. Especially since, as I told you, if we go to trial, I'll dismiss the D.C. and proceed on the obstructing and bail-jumping. I'll get two nine-month misdemeanor convictions. *[Beat.]* But I agree a trial's a lot of trouble, and I have too many cases *[He gestures around.]* to spend more than five minutes on the insignificant ones, the ones that don't make the headlines. Thirty days plus the fine, did I hear you say?

136

That's not enough. Forty-five plus the fine or sixty without.
Take it or leave it.

*[The attorney glances over at Pat, who has a blank
expression.]*

ATTORNEY
We'll take it, one or the other. Put the offer down in your
notes in case you're not there and somebody else from your
office handles it. Schedule it for a plea. And make sure we
get a notice of the court date this time.

ASSISTANT DISTRICT ATTORNEY
Certified mail?

ATTORNEY
Yeah.

*[The attorney gets up, Pat follows, and they walk out.
Blackout.]*

Scene 17. Pat's and Sam's Home

[The stage is dark. Lights partially up on the left half of the stage. Some movement may be seen and heard onstage, which is Pat stirring.]

PAT
Is that you? *[Pat turns on a lamp and looks around. Pat has been sleeping on the sofa.]* Sam, are you home? *[Pat sits motionless for a moment, picks up the clock, looks at the time, and sets it down again. After another moment of indecision, Pat stands up, turn on the room lights -- at which the lights go fully up on the left side of stage -- picks up the phone, looks at a number affixed to the side, and dials.]* Hello. No, this is not an emergency. At least I hope not, but ... OK, I can hold. Hello. I called a couple of hours ago ... Well, can you just tell me if you've had any reports of ... *[Sam has approached the door and now makes some noise opening it.]* Wait. Oh, it's OK, she's home now. Thanks anyway. Bye. *[Pat hangs up and jumps up as Sam comes through the door.]* You're home. Are you okay?

SAM
Yeah, I'm okay.

PAT
I was worried about you. I called the police every hour or so.

SAM
I'm sorry.

PAT
Where were you.

138

SAM

At the party, Robin's party. Don't you remember?

PAT

So you did go there.

SAM

Of course. I told you that.

PAT

Did you stay there all night?

SAM

Nah. When Robin started looking at the clock, we left and continued the party elsewhere.

PAT

Who is "we".

SAM

Seven of us. People I met at the party. You wouldn't know them. We had a wonderful time. I drove all of us around town, we stopped at a bar for awhile, celebrated the Badger's *[Choose a sports team of local interest, preferably one with a fight song.]* victory, drove around some more, stopped at a truck stop for an early breakfast, and drove to Olin Park to watch the sun rise. We talked and talked, and solved everybody's problems, our own and the world's. It was so much fun.

PAT

You drove?

SAM

I was careful. I only had one or two drinks at each place.

PAT
You could've called.

SAM
I was hoping you were asleep and I didn't want to wake you.

PAT
Not bother me!? You think I wasn't bothered all night!?

SAM
So?!

PAT
OK, so I did that, too. But I've been getting nothing but grief
ever since that night, so I think I'm justified in giving you
some too, and getting some answers. What were these
people's names, if there really were seven of you.

SAM
What is this about me giving you grief! You think I've given
you grief? I think I've been exceptionally, not to say
absurdly, non-confrontational about your escapade that
landed
you in somebody's face and maybe in somebody's bed and
maybe yet in jail. I don't think I need to tell you anything
more until you tell me what you did that night. At least I
managed to get through the night without a criminal charge.

[Pat grabs Sam's jacket.]

PAT
You did this on purpose!

[Sam yanks her clothing out of Pat's hand and Pat raises his

hand to strike Sam.]

SAM
Let go of me! Don't you dare hit me! If you do, the police'll have you out of here so fast your head'll spin. And then I swear you'll never see me again.

PAT
I --

SAM
Maybe we'd better continue this discussion after you've calmed down a little. I'm going to use the bathroom.

[Sam exits through the left door to the bathroom area offstage. Pat stands motionless. The noise of water running starts, then stops. There is a knock at the front door.]

PAT
Just a minute! *[Pat goes to the door and opens it. The same police officer enters.]* Good morning, officer. You must have traced my call. It's okay now, really. My wife came home safely. I'm pretty pissed that she stayed out all night, but at least she's home safely now.

POLICE OFFICER
What call was that, sir.

PAT
Isn't that why you're here, because I called?

[Sound of a toilet flushing.]

POLICE OFFICER
I'm afraid it's not. Did you call the police?

141

PAT

Yes. I was worried when my wife didn't come home, but it's okay. She's here now.

POLICE OFFICER

I see. Well, that's fortunate, because I need to talk to her.

PAT

Did she get into some sort of trouble last night?

POLICE OFFICER

Did she?

PAT

I don't know. I just know that she was out all night.

SAM

Who are you talking to?

PAT

A cop. She wants to talk to you.

[Sam enters.]

SAM

Good morning, officer. Did something happen last night? I really don't remember seeing anything unusual, but if you can tell me what you're after, maybe I'll be able to remember something.

POLICE OFFICER

Do you own a blue Cavalier, *[Choose an inexpensive car.]* license number DGC636?

SAM
Yes.

POLICE OFFICER
Were you driving it at around 2:45 this morning?

SAM
Yes, I was.

POLICE OFFICER
We received a complaint against you.

SAM
For what.

POLICE OFFICER
Apparently you and a number of other people in the car were singing "On Wisconsin" *[Choose a local variant.]* a little too loudly in a residential area.

SAM
Oh, I'm sorry. I know you're right. Are you going to give me a ticket?

POLICE OFFICER
Can I assume it won't happen again?

SAM
Absolutely, officer. Scout's honor.

POLICE OFFICER
Then I can let you off with a warning, this time.

SAM
Thank you so much.

POLICE OFFICER
By the way, how many of you were in that car.

SAM
Uh, seven. Why do you ask. Is there a legal limit?

POLICE OFFICER
Not really, except for seatbelts. It's just that the person who called mentioned something about four-part harmony. Keep it down next time.

SAM
There won't be a next time. Thank you again, officer.

POLICE OFFICER
You're welcome. Good-bye.

SAM
Good-bye.

[The police officer leaves. Pat and Sam look at each other. Sam sticks out her tongue and leaves. Lights down.]

Scene 18. The Courtroom

[Lights up on the right half of the stage, which is again the courtroom. The only persons on stage are the attorney, the A.D.A., and the First Denizen cringeing on a bench in a corner. The attorney leaps up as Pat walks in.]

ATTORNEY
There you are. I'm glad you're early. Maybe we can get in right away, and save some time. Here, fill out this plea questionnaire. I'll tell the clerk we're ready and get in first.

PAT
What if I don't understand something here.

ATTORNEY
Do the best you can. If you really don't understand, ask me when I come back and I'll explain it to you.

[The attorney leaves. Pat sits and looks at the paper for a moment.]

PAT
Could you explain something really simple to me.

ASSISTANT DISTRICT ATTORNEY
Absolutely not. I can't talk to you without your attorney present.

PAT
Sorry. *[He turns to the denizen.]* You'll probably know this.

FIRST DENIZEN
I can't deal with anybody's problems but my own today.

145

But say, did you hear the one about the argument between the doctor, the engineer and the lawyer over whose profession's the oldest?

[Pause.]

PAT
No.

FIRST DENIZEN
The doctor said medicine's the oldest 'cause god created Eve out of Adam's rib. The engineer said engineering's older 'cause even before Adam and Eve, god created order out of chaos. But the lawyer won the argument by saying "and who do you think created chaos?"

[Pat returns to work on the form.]

PAT
Am I making this plea voluntarily.

[Beat. Pat closes his eyes and leans his forehead on his hand a while, then raises and shakes his head, and returns to the task of checking boxes. The attorney returns.]

ATTORNEY
We're set. She'll be right in. It'll only take a minute. Did you finish?

PAT
Well ...

ATTORNEY
Well?

PAT
Yes. *[He checks a final box and hands it to the attorney.]*
Here.

ATTORNEY
Good.

[One of the functionaries intones "All rise." Pat and the denizen stand up. The attorney and the ADA half-rise and sit down again. The judge enters and sits.]

JUDGE
Be seated. *[Pat and the denizen sit.]* Mimi ni kisu, wewe nyama. Yeye ni mwewa, wao ni wabaya. Ms. Gunther, please approach the bench. I must tell you what Attorney Labreche did yesterday after you left court. *[The judge motions to the A.D.A., who goes forward. The judge whispers and the A.D.A. laughs.]* Can you believe that?

ASSISTANT DISTRICT ATTORNEY
Only he could do that.

JUDGE
Well if he does it again, I'll cite him for contempt and arrest his butt. You may return to your seat. *[The A.D.A. does.]* State versus Samuel Taylor. Scheduled for trial to the court.

FIRST DENIZEN
Here, your honor.

ATTORNEY
But I thought we were next.

JUDGE
You were mistaken. My clerk told me someone has been

147

sitting here in the courtroom all day. Has that been you?

FIRST DENIZEN
Yes, you honor. I've been here since the doors opened at
seven A.M.

JUDGE
Admirable. Ms. Gunther, are you ready to proceed?

ASSISTANT DISTRICT ATTORNEY
Yes.

JUDGE
And Mr. Taylor, are your witnesses here? Are you ready to
proceed?

FIRST DENIZEN
My witnesses said they wouldn't come to court no more.
They already lost two days pay sitting here.

JUDGE
Then we'll set another date and I'll order them to appear for
you. Ms. Gunther will issue subpoenas for the court. What
are their names.

FIRST DENIZEN
If you please, your honor. I'd rather just go ahead and get it
over with today. My witnesses would've told you I wasn't
driving, but I'd rather just plead guilty.

JUDGE
I'll ignore your unsolicited remark about what the witnesses
would have said, and strike it from the record. Do not try to
influence the court again, Mr. Taylor. What will you be
recommending for a sentence, Ms. Gunther?

ASSISTANT DISTRICT ATTORNEY
Five days in jail, satisfied by time already served. He was
incarcerated for eight days on a warrant before he posted the
thousand dollars bond.

JUDGE
Have you filled out a plea questionnaire, and do you
understand all the rights you are giving up by your plea?

FIRST DENIZEN
Yes, your honor.

JUDGE
Bring it up here. *[The denizen stands, approaches the judge,
hands her a paper, and
returns to his seat. The judge gives it a cursory glance.]* Is
there anything you wish to say before I pass sentence upon
you?

FIRST DENIZEN
Well, I lost my job because –

JUDGE
That is of no legal consequence. Anything else?

FIRST DENIZEN
Only that ... No, your honor.

JUDGE
Then I find you guilty of driving a vehicle after your license
was suspended, and I sentence you to eight days in the
county jail, with credit for five days already served. Report
to the jail immediately to serve the remaining three days.
The paperwork will be there shortly. *[The denizen looks at*

the A.D.A. and the judge, and then shuffles toward the door.]

FIRST DENIZEN
Say, how can you tell when an attorney's lying. *[Beat.]* Her
lips are moving.

[The denizen shuffles out.]

JUDGE
State versus Pat Barlow. Scheduled for a plea. Is this your
client, Ms. Smith?

ATTORNEY
Yes.

JUDGE
Ms. Gunther, what is your recommendation for sentence.

ASSISTANT DISTRICT ATTORNEY
The state moves to dismiss the disorderly conduct and bail-
jumping charges, and Mr. Barlow will plead other than not
guilty to the remaining charge of obstruction of justice.
There will then be a joint recommendation for sixty days in
jail.

JUDGE
Is that so, Ms. Smith?

ATTORNEY
Yes, your honor.

PAT
[Sotto voce.] What is this new one: not other than guilty? Is
that what I have to say?

ATTORNEY
[Whispers back.] Yes.

PAT
What does it mean.

JUDGE
Is that your plea, Mr. Barlow?

[Pat looks wildly at his attorney.]

PAT
[Sotto voce.] Is it?

JUDGE
Mr. Barlow, is that your plea!?

[Pat looks at the attorney, who nods.]

PAT
Yes!

JUDGE
I thought you told me this case was ready. The court must
inform all parties that it does not appreciate games being
played. Next time, Ms. Smith, do it right. Did you complete
a plea questionnaire and do you understand all the rights you
are giving up by your plea?

PAT
[After a slight hesitation, but galvanized by the thought of
the judge yelling again.] Yes!

151

JUDGE
Then upon your plea this court finds you guilty of a violation of section nine-forty-six, point forty-one of the statutes, and it is the judgment of this court that you be sentenced to six days in the county jail and a six thousand dollar fine. When should the sentence commence.

ASSISTANT DISTRICT ATTORNEY
The most convenient time for the jail staff is Tuesday morning, after the weekend detainees have gone to court and been released on Monday.

JUDGE
Then you are to report to the jail next Tuesday morning. What time.

ASSISTANT DISTRICT ATTORNEY
I don't think it makes a difference. How about 8 A.M.

JUDGE
Next Tuesday at 8 A.M. And if you are not there at that time, a warrant will issue for your arrest, and you will be picked up at a time which is considerably less convenient for you. Case adjourned.

[The lights on the stage go down.]

Scene 19. Pat's and Sam's Home

[Pat enters the apartment through the front door. On the floor is an envelope, which he picks up and opens. He takes out a sheet of paper and appears to read it as the words are read offstage.]

SAM

Good-bye. I am now certain that something did happen that night, and it shows a side of you that I don't know and don't want to know. I'm surprised, and relieved, that you were only charged with disorderly conduct instead of something more serious. I also know I can't trust you. It's over between us. I don't intend to give you another opportunity to lay your hands on me in anger. Every relationship, like every thing, has a breaking point, and when that breaking point is reached, all the energy and effort that went into holding it together vanishes. I've taken all the things I care about. Don't come looking for me.

[He exits through the back door for a moment and returns with a small backpack, then he exits through the front door and walks down from the stage into the theater. If possible, he walks up an aisle, across the back of the theater, and back down the other aisle, eventually sinking down into a seat in the front row of the audience.]

153

Scene 20. The Processing Area of a Jail

[Lights up on the right side of the stage, which now shows a desk and chair and a cell door. Pat gets up from his seat and goes onto the set. The First Denizen enters.]

FIRST DENIZEN
Ave, verum corpus.

PAT
What? Oh, hello.

FIRST DENIZEN
I didn't expect to see you here, but I've learned not to expect anything in this madhouse except the unexpected and the incomprehensible. Say, how can you tell when your attorney puts her interest above yours.

PAT
Uh, I don't know.

FIRST DENIZEN
I think you do by now. She's an attorney.

[The Jailer enters and sits at the desk, looking as outrageous as possible.]

JAILER *[to the First Denizen]*
Why are you here?

FIRST DENIZEN
I know my order says Thursday but I was hoping I could start early.

154

JAILER
Start a sentence early!? Why.

FIRST DENIZEN
I lost my job and now I'm homeless, so ...

JAILER
You expected us to give you free room and board? Ha!

FIRST DENIZEN
I really have nowhere else to go except to be on the street.

JAILER
Too bad! Get out! Come back when you've been ordered
to.

FIRST DENIZEN
Just don't trip over me when you leave the building today.

[The First Denizen exits.]

JAILER
And who are you.

PAT
Barlow. Pat Barlow.

*[The Jailer looks in a ledger. Pat approaches the desk,
carrying the backpack. The Police Officer, the Detective,
the D.A., the Judge, and the Attorney enter, dance across the
stage hand-in-hand, and either exit across the stage or stand
behind the Jailer.]*

 JAILER
Sixteen days and six hundred dollars.

PAT
Uh, it's supposed to be six days.

JAILER
That's not what the order says. Sixteen days. Drop the
backpack. Take a step back.

[Pat sets the backpack down and steps back.]

JAILER
I'll take that.

*[The Jailer approaches, picks up the backpack, places it on
the desk, and unzips it.]*

JAILER
Strip.

*[After a moment, Pat begins to disrobe, which can go as far
as the director chooses. Lights down.]*

END OF PLAY

Author's Notes

The set and characters in the first scene should be realistic.
Starting with scene two, sets and characters should acquire
increasingly unrealistic, surrealistic, and expressionistic
touches, culminating in truly bizarre visual, auditory, and
other effects. Among the possibilities are masks, amplified
or distorted voices, cue cards, or theatre effects from other
traditions, such as Noh or puppet theater (shadow puppets,
bunraku puppets, punch and judy puppets). The author
encourages the director's creativity, and such effects are left
to the director's imagination and resources. The play is
intended to sound current and local, so references to
vehicles, television shows, etc. should be updated, and the
names of recognizable local personalities may be used for
the incidental characters.

The Second Attorney's statement in scene 6 is a saying
attributed to Abraham Lincoln, "He can compress the most
words into the smallest ideas better than any man I ever
met."
The Judge's statement in scene 8 is derived from Anatole
France's saying, "The law, in its majestic equality, forbids
the rich as well as the poor to sleep under bridges, to beg in
the streets, and to steal bread."

My only acknowledgement to Franz Kafka's The Trial is
that it greatly hindered my writing. Once the idea for this
play arose, I assumed that it would be in danger of being
derivative. The parallels to Kafka were unavoidable, but they
are a different artist's reaction to the justice system itself,
and if anything, the constant echoes of The Trial made the
writing of this work more difficult.

First Staged Reading – October 2001
Pat Barlow [Steve Edelstein]
Sam [Julie Kean]
Police Officer [Matt Spring]
Police Receptionist [Erika Kirchberg]
Detective Perez [Bob Curry]
Courtroom Denizen [Patrick Barlow]
Judge [Sandy Adell]
Public Defender Receptionist [Katherine Sainsbury]
First Attorney in P.D.'s Office [Heather Wright]
Second Attorney in P.D.'s Office [Laura Wendt]
Assistant District Attorney [Kathryn Ambler]

Second Staged Reading – February 2002
Pat Barlow [Bryan Hubrecht]
Sam [Portia Adney]
Police Officer and First Denizen [Jessie Clements]
Police Receptionist, Public Defender Receptionist, and
Second Denizen [Vicki Williams]
Detective Perez and Assistant District Attorney [Lorna
Ringlund]
Judge [Donna Rae Clasen]
First Attorney in P.D.'s Office and Attorney [Betty
Diamond]
Second Attorney in P.D.'s Office and Second Attorney
[Kyle Konop]
Director [Rauel Labreche]
Stage Manager [Rebecca Borlaug]

www.ingramcontent.com/pod-product-compliance
Lightning Source LLC
Chambersburg PA
CBHW051902090426

42811CB00003B/433